The Extra Mile

A Celebration Of People

André Bernier

Contents

Foreword

Because this book is not really about me but the people who have, in some way, changed my life for the better, you will see many names within the pages of this book. Eventually, you may have noticed something peculiar. Except where the storyline insisted, my immediate family members are mostly in the background, and that is by design. Because I am a public figure in a large television market, I actively protect my family's privacy. They are not on television and radio, and they have no desire to be. Even though my wife, son, parents, siblings, and extended relatives played a major role in shaping the person I became, it was my desire to respect those special family moments by revering them as hallowed ground.

If our paths have crossed over the course of my half-century journey and your name is not mentioned in the main content of the book, this is where I will allow myself the luxury of hopefully mentioning you here.

This book is divided into seven chapters. Each chapter covers a specific time period or place in chronological order:

Chapter 1: Joe Belmore, Mémere Dorée, Sister Cecile at the Marian Manor, Mimi LeBlanc, The Dahlbergs, "Shorty," the Moniz

Family, Henry and Betty Blackburn, Mr. Griffin, Lorrie Barnes, Arnold Ziffle, Richard Dunn.

Chapter 2: George Biscari, Diane Beaulieu Gendron, Rick Khuner, Vicki Alves Crapo, Lynne Cotter, Robert Gomes, Roberta Dupree, Debbie Gauthier, John and Andrew Gounaris, Mario Cardoza, Alan Soares, Dr. Normand E. Olivier, Joe Winterhalter Sr. and Jr., Connie Grimes, Tom Hardman, Cliff Irwin, Bob Copeland, John Parisi.

Chapter 3: Theresa Souza, Carl and Janice St. Pierre, Dr. John Muzzey, Dr. Michael Sherbrooke, Arthur Steinberg, Norm Sebastian, Marcia Rumsey Whitaker, Joe Marcello, Darlene Periconi, Kevin Kennedy, Dawn Kennedy Manausa, Nick Gregory, Kathy Perbeck Lucas, Carolyn Schenck Basierbe, Eric Scher, Jeff Herbeck, Jeff Lyons, Barbara Konrad, Steve Noguiera, Steve Caporizzo, Peter DiAngelo, Don Murray, Jim Van Kovics, John Guaraldi, John DeBlock, Todd Gross, Tom Chisolm.

Chapter 4: Gene Lively, Wally Peterson, Rick Sellers, Chris Legeros, Steve Jackson, Lee Dennis, Barry Norris, Nancy Bruce, Bob Bruner, Maggie Jenson, Jeff Kennedy.

Chapter 5: Scotty Lancaster, Bill Keneely, Herb Stevens, Al Lipson, Craig Weber, Will Annen, Dale Bryan, Jim Wegner.

Chapter 6: Frank Stackowitz, Mike Jacobsen, Mario Impagliazzo, Nick Lawler, Chris Wheeler, John Bachman, Robert Vanatta.

Chapter 7: Denise Dufala, Rick Young, Danny Coughlin, Bill Martin, Stacey Bell, Stephanie Schaefer, Wayne Dawson, Dwayne Dawson, Greg Pike, Merle and Judy Schwartz, Morris

Eason, John and Sandee Spisak, Mary Woisnet, Garland Likins, Rick Parkin, Firman and Key Pope, Russ and Joyce Kallay, Bruce Dilling, Angie Warrington, A. J. Colby, Rev. Anthony Marshall, Dick Russ, Loree Vick, Chet Roberts, Mark Koontz, Bob Cerminera, Kelly O'Donnell, Dympna Jacobsen, Florin and Heather Weber Stan, Danielle von Loewe, Cal O'Kelly, Jim and Michelle Caputo, John Ghiorse, Don Kent, Paul Carter, Gary Bittner, Mark Zimmerman, Jan Markowitz, Tom Bishop, Ed Bostic, Brian Brooks, Terry Hunka, Suzie Thomas, Lin McDowell, Audrey Rinicella, Stephen Burks, Dave Lynden, Marlene Renner, Greg Easterly, Sonya Thompson, Andy Fishman, Jeff Fitch, Tony Hurst, Marc McKee, Rob and Kinney Cathcart, Joel and Rhonda Rudicil, P. J. Meduri, Clarence Byrd, Claude Williams, Steve Sawczak.

Invariably, I will forget to include someone whose name should have appeared here but that will never diminish your significance from within the framework of my life's journey. I shall forever love each and every single one of you.

Introduction

In March of 1992, I corralled a friend, Brad England, to drive with me to Pittsburgh to take in a live performance of "A Prairie Home Companion." Being Garrison Keillor fans, we had both always wanted to see one of his live radio broadcasts in person. We were not disappointed. Pittsburgh was an enchanting city, and Heinz Auditorium was simply breathtaking. During the two-hour program, the famous Fred Rogers from "Mr. Rogers' Neighborhood" suddenly appeared on stage. What a delight! Both Brad and I were immediately endeared by this gentle giant of public television.

When "Mr. Rogers' Neighborhood" began airing on PBS in 1969, I was ten years old. Despite being a little older than the intended target audience, I found that I enjoyed watching the program with my younger brother. There was just something about the way he made you feel personally welcomed that kept me quietly and casually watching every now and then.

Through the years, I've enjoyed the literature that was either authored by him or written about him. The more I read, the more I saw that Fred Rogers' interest in all people was beyond genuine. What you saw on television is who Fred Rogers was in everyday life. Aside from seeing him on stage in Pittsburgh, I never met him personally but with every book I read by or about Mr. Rogers, I felt as if I was reading about an intimate, old friend whom I had known a lifetime.

The most recent book that I downloaded from iTunes was an audio book by Texas print journalist Tim Madigan. The book title is *I'm Proud Of You - My Friendship With Fred Rogers*. In it, Tim mentioned that when Fred was invited to speak anywhere he would invariably ask the audience to close their eyes and remain silent while thinking about the people in their lives who made them who they are. Each time, the room became pin-dropping silent in the exercise. Some of his audience might have been thinking about this for the very first time. It's not hard imagining that each person marveled at the personal investments that others had made in them along life's journey.

I found this exercise a fascinating one. It's one I have casually done over the years usually as a moment of reminiscing about someone who had extended great kindness or acceptance to me. If that certain someone was no longer alive, I would occasionally even stop to thank God for sending this individual into my life and ask if possible to let them know beyond the eternal curtain how grateful I am for them. But I have never taken a collective landscape look at all the people who made sacrificial investments into my life, all at once, in one minute. In fact, it could not be done. On a yellow legal pad, I began writing the names of those special people. One minute turned into five. Five turned into sixty. The more I thought about it, the more it consumed me. For those who will grant me more time, this book will do the topic much more justice.

It's really more than just a book about other people. It's an autobiographical sketch in a relational timeline format paying honor to those people who have helped me to become who I am.

In the Gospel of Luke, Jesus spoke about what you should do if asked to walk with someone for a mile. During the Roman occupation of the Holy Land during Jesus' ministry on Earth, it was not uncommon for a tired Roman soldier to randomly select a native Jew to demand that he carry his gear for a mile. While doing so was compulsory it was obviously not the kind of task that was done with a great deal of eagerness. Jesus challenged His followers to quite a paradigm shift. He said that the one who was asked to walk a mile should go two! This is where we get the phrase, "to go the extra mile."

Most of us walk the mile required of us in our daily schedule. We work, care for our families and maintain our friendships. In some cases walking the required mile barely keeps our heads above water. But there is an interesting group that seems to thrive on going the extra mile. Oddly it's the extra mile that seems to pull them out of the raging river of life. They run along the shoreline and enjoy the scenery all the while. Those that made the biggest impact in my life walked the extra mile in order to make an investment in me. They didn't do so out of obligation. Instead they were fueled by the joy they received from pouring into someone else.

Whether it was for only a few steps or for twenty miles, everyone with whom I have enjoyed walking through life has had a part in molding me. God has placed each person into my life for very specific seasons of my journey for which I will be eternally grateful.

Chapter 1

Head In The Clouds

A Divine Gift Of Passion

I was born to a father and mother that were both of French-Canadian heritage and both very fluent in both French and English. They thought it would be advantageous for me to learn French first. For the first four years of my life, I spoke primarily French. Most of the time it was not an issue or problem since the vast majority of our family and community spoke French. For many decades in the 1900s, New Bedford was well known for its rich French-Canadian culture.

Paul Lemaire was born within days of me at New Bedford's St. Luke's Hospital. That's when my mother befriended Paul's mother, Rita. As Paul and I grew from infants to toddlers, our families got to know each other quite well. After my brother Denié was born, we called her "Aunty Rita" and Paul called our mother, "Aunty Claire."

As my parents told the story ad nauseam but to my amusement, I was about three or four years old when Aunt Rita and Paul were over for a visit. We were busy playing with trucks in a pile of dirt near the tall pine tree in the backyard. I spoke French. Paul spoke English. It was not an issue. We were quite content moving trucks around in the dirt using the universal language of truck engine sounds as both mothers enjoyed each other's company nearby.

It was your typical warm summer afternoon with a sticky breeze. Somehow, I caught a glimpse of something that grabbed my attention. I stopped playing with the trucks and stood up, looking over the neighbor's fence. After Paul noticed I had stopped playing with our trucks, he too stood up and looked in the same direction. An approaching summer thunderstorm had made the sky color alarmingly unfriendly and I had noticed it.

Finally pointing toward the chaotic sky, I proclaimed, "Regarde! Les nuages noirs!"

Paul pointed out to the same sky and said, "No. Black clouds."

"Non! Les nuages noirs!"

"No! Black clouds!"

As the argument began heating up, the two Moms came over to find out what the problem was. It didn't take too long for them to discover that not only were Paul and I pointing to the same thing, but we were also saying the same thing as well. In French, black cloud is nuage noir. Apparently, whatever our mothers did to diffuse the argument worked and life went on as normal, or so my parents thought.

For days and then weeks after that event, I began looking at the sky every day and asking what the outside temperature was. As if it changed minute by minute, I would ask dozens of times every day. Being fascinated with numbers of all sorts, I would also ask about the time and anything else expressed as a number. My mother told me that she had to remind herself not to get frustrated with the continuous questions and to be thankful for each teachable moment. Her assumption was that the questions would disappear after a season, so she entertained them. That assumption slowly disappeared like deep mountain snow pack in March and April.

In hindsight, there isn't a single moment of my life where I can remember wanting to pursue anything else. Weather was much more than a passion. While I certainly did not recognize it when I was a young boy, hindsight has shown me clearly that it was a Divine gift that fueled my journey from the get-go. It's a gift I will always treasure no matter where the Lord leads me on the road that is yet to be traveled on this side of eternity.

School Bell

The first few years of school for me were a bit of a blur although certainly there are moments that I remember as clearly as though they happened yesterday.

I started school at St. Anthony's, a parochial K-12 school about a mile from our house. While our family officially were congregants of Sacred Heart Church, we would often go to St. Anthony's to attend services. Both families on my father's and mother's side knew the clergy there very well because of my grandfather, Damase, who was St. Anthony's caretaker for decades.

I remember my kindergarten teacher, Mrs. Berger. Yes, you probably guessed right. Many of us called her Mrs. Hamburger but it truly was a term of endearment. She was key in assimilating me into English since she spoke both French and English well.

I'll never forget my first day of school. Naturally my mother was exceedingly curious as to what I was feeling and thinking. I rather enjoyed my first day there and found Mrs. Berger to be very pleasant. But Mom had an odd look on her face when I told her that she greeted the class and told everyone "to be forbidden." After a careful debriefing, Mom was able to determine that Mrs. Berger told us all to "be seated." Big difference.

I quickly made friends with a girl in my class. Her name was Elizabeth and she was a cutie. Her brother, Joseph, also went to school there and we used to often walk past my Aunt Georgette's Fish N' Chips restaurant on Acushnet Avenue only two blocks from the school. They were on their way home while I walked to the Fish N' Chips to meet up with my mother who was waiting for me there. For several weeks after, she would see Elizabeth and me walking hand-in-hand by the window of the restaurant before I came in the door and they continued to their home. She finally asked me about this. While I have no idea why I would conjure up such a tall tale, I told her that every boy was assigned a girlfriend at the beginning of the year and that Elizabeth was the one to whom I was assigned. I revealed this just before the parent-teacher conference night and I suddenly was terrified at the prospect of having my bluff called. In hindsight, the story I spun was hilarious. Mom's look of disapproval was all I needed to know that while she found the story amusing, she knew it was not truthful. Nonetheless, she gave me grace and elbow room to learn from telling such wild stories.

My imagination did serve me well with one early assignment. It was to write about something that I would personally like to invent. Because I was fascinated with numbers, and since digital watches did not yet exist, my invention was a digital watch whose digits would glow just like the time and temperature signs I would see at banks. The only difference was that the digits would glow red during the day and green at night. The approval for such an elaborate invention from my second grade teacher was satisfying. Three years later, I saw my invention on my Uncle Roland's wrist. The digital watch had bright red digits that would display the time when you pushed a button on the frame. While the digits did not change color at sundown, I still wondered how a watchmaker could have possibly stolen my idea for this newfangled watch.

You would think that as one gets older, the more you are likely to remember about school. Oddly enough, aside from my invention assignment, I do not remember first or second grade nearly as clearly as I do kindergarten. The only memory that remains of those years is the kindness of a nun whose name was phonetically the same as mine, Sister Andrée, who looked after me in the courtyard during recess. I thought it was different to have a nun whose name was the same as mine. I would call to her by the name, "Andrée" without the proper title of "Sister." Most students would get knuckled by a ruler for that, but not with Sister Andrée. She showed me a great deal of compassion and grace and simply pulled me aside and whispered in my ear, "don't forget the 'Sister' part, OK?"

Miss Sanchez

By the time I started third grade and my brother first grade, our parents moved us to Mt. Pleasant Elementary, a public school which is within eyeshot of the front room window of the home in which we grew up. Since the class stayed together from year to year until we graduated from elementary school, I still remember many of my classmates' names along with their youthful faces.

Most of them were just classroom acquaintances, while slightly deeper friendships formed with others - Cynthia Reynolds, Tom Landry, Richard Dunn, Kathy Helgeland (whose younger brother, Brian, is now a famous Hollywood movie screenwriter) and Kathy Dziuba, a girl on whom I had a quiet and long-lasting crush that lasted for years. Then there was my neighbor friend, Jim Buckley. Jim lived across the street on 87 Sutton Street and because we were born only days apart from each other, we were practically inseparable. Jim is one of the few elementary school friends with whom I am still in regular contact.

Aside from the names and faces of classmates and my extended family, the only others who made any kind of indelible mark on me at this stage in life's journey were a handful of special teachers.

Miss Sanchez was one of our regular substitute teachers at Mt. Pleasant. She was perceivably closer to her senior years compared to the regular teaching staff but never lacking in energy or maintaining a level of respect from all of us. She was thin and her skin was wrinkly and gently olive-toned. Her hair was a bristly salt-and-pepper mop that she kept tied back in a bun. It looked like it might be the only way she could wear it without beginning to have hair that looked like Don King.

Granted, there is just so much you can do as a substitute teacher other than to follow the teacher's plan. Getting to know students well was not really one of them. That did not discourage Miss Sanchez from trying.

Just exactly how she was able to find out that I loved anything to do with the weather, sky and numbers is still beyond me. That resonated with her since she was interested in astronomy. At one point during one of her fill-ins as our substitute teacher, she asked me up to her desk. She said that she had something for me. Miss Sanchez introduced me to the *Old Farmer's Almanac*. It not only had their famous long-range weather predictions, but intriguing sunrise and sunset tables for every month of the year for Boston. It also had interesting astronomy articles that she pointed out. Wanting to impress her that I knew something about astronomy, I told her that I was aware that Cassiopeia would be visible for the first time in a long time. Her eyebrows went up as if to express interest as she encouraged me to take the books and to learn more from them. Miss Sanchez could have easily popped my bubble and let me know that the constellation Cassiopeia is a circumpolar constellation and is always visible at our latitude. Knowing that it would have splashed cold water on my interest and being the real encourager that she was, she let me eventually discover that and much more on my own.

Miss Burke

I find it ironic and humorous that, as I was writing this chapter, I received an out-of-the-blue email from one of my classmates from the Mt. Pleasant Elementary school era. Just as I am still curious about the whereabouts and life stories of all of them, Cynthia Reynolds beat me to the punch by finding me. I'm not a proponent of what the world calls coincidence. God directs our paths in such delightfully detailed ways. Cyndi's email was Divinely timed. Since I was not able to remember the teachers we had in the third and fourth grades, I asked her if she remembered. Less than a day later, Cyndi gave me the list since her mother saved all of her report cards. They were:

3rd Grade – Miss Pinheiro

4th Grade – Miss Erikson (who became Mrs. Harrison that year)

5th Grade – Miss Burke

6th Grade – Mr. DePrato

In 1969 we all moved to the fifth grade classroom on the third floor of Mt. Pleasant Elementary with Miss Burke. Tom Landry was still the strongest kid in the class who was always picked as one of the team captains in kickball at recess. Jim Buckley was still the smartest boy in the class and my best friend, and Kathy Dziuba still made my palms sweaty. Milk was still a nickel and peanut butter crackers a dime for our mid-morning snack. Mr. Door, a towering hulk who was over six feet tall, was still our gym teacher twice a week. We all learned together, worked together, played together and laughed together.

Miss Burke was a large woman who was always smiling. If she wasn't wearing her smile on the outside there was plenty of evidence of it showing on the inside. While her voice may have sounded shrilling and tinny at times, her spirit was bubbly with joy and she always sought to bring out the best in each of us no matter where we were at academically or socially.

She was quite an accomplished pianist which is very likely why hers was the only classroom that I can remember that ever had a piano in it. The piano was on the left side of her desk close to the windows which had a western view overlooking the schoolyard. At least three times a week, the lesson plan book suddenly closed and she would stroll over to the piano and tell everyone to pull out and open their song books. Most of the time she would let us pick the songs that she would play and we would sing.

There was one particular classmate who, when recognized, we would all hold our collective breaths and pray he would not pick the song that he liked to sing. As reliable as the atomic clock in Boulder, Colorado, he always asked if we could sing, "Little Red Caboose." Ugh. It wasn't so much the song itself that bothered most of us but rather it was the final, non-musical exclamation that made me and many others cringe.

"Choooooooooooo! Choooooooooooo!"

Fifth graders simply don't do that. Yet Miss Burke always validated every student's personal tastes and choices by honoring them unconditionally. It's no wonder she was well liked by all of us even if she insisted we all sing the song that most of us wanted to rip out of our song books.

Having me in a classroom with windows was dangerous. Since weather fascinated me, I was always checking on what was happening outside. It went far beyond a casual glance. To the detriment of my class work, I'd analyze everything from how the wind was moving the flag to watching clouds. If it was raining or, worse yet, snowing, my analysis would become nothing short of obsessive. This put me in a pickle more than once if I was called on to participate in an oral exercise.

I can remember Miss Burke teaching a new mathematical principle of some sort one day and the weather happening just outside that long row of windows was far too interesting to want to pay attention. Wouldn't you know that my name came up in her stack of random cards. She asked me a question and I simply shrugged my shoulders and gave her a deer-in-headlights look. With patience and grace, she tried to walk me through the logic of the question, but when she asked for the final answer, I gave her an answer that was not even close to being correct. Very methodically she tried again. I did all right until she asked for the final answer. But because my mind was captivated by the neat clouds and not the new concept, I gave her the same incorrect answer as before. Disgusted but not discouraged, she tried yet one more time but we ended up in the same place. Despite many similar episodes, she never gave up on trying to get my mind out of "daydreaming" mode. What she did not know was that I was not daydreaming at all. My mind was actively engaged in the academics of watching live meteorological phenomena.

Little did I know that I was in good company. Decades earlier, Don Kent, the dean of New England television weather, found himself in the same situation during his elementary school days. Twenty years after Don's retirement from television in 1983, he invited Eric Pinder and Sarah Long to his New Hampshire home for an extensive interview for his web site. In the on-line article, Don recalled his years in his third grade classroom:

"The teacher had wondered why I wanted to sit in the back in the corner and look out the window all the time and not pay attention," he recalls with a laugh, seventy-six years later. He finally told her that he was watching the weather—"Which way the flag is going and all the rest." With his teacher's cooperation, he started writing the forecast on the classroom's chalkboard every day. "That's how I became the weatherman, the third grade weatherman."

As spring arrived it was time to take our class photograph. When the day arrived, my mother made certain that I would be wearing something that would look stately and timeless. A light-colored turtleneck with a brown suit jacket did the trick. That week, I did everything in my power to straighten my hopelessly curly hair and I met with only a limited amount of success. (It wasn't until I was in high school that the "afro" came into style and I discovered that I was the envy of those who had straight hair.)

A few weeks passed before the photo packets arrived for us to take home to our parents. Miss Burke began passing them out walking past each student's desk. When she came to my desk, she stopped and pulled out my photo.

"I must say, André, that you have the most wonderful smile," she exclaimed in front of all my classmates.

"Your smile is just like that of a Hollywood movie star. It's a wonderful photo. Very nice."

Her words still ring in my memory like they were spoken only days ago. They were words of affirmation and encouragement in a fifth-grade world where each classmate was trying to find a way to stand out. Unknowingly, Miss Burke gave me the thumbs-up to press on to my goal. Maybe, just maybe, my dream wasn't a futile grasp at the stars. But before I took that calculated swipe, I had to tackle sixth grade first.

We all slid down a few rooms to Mr. DePrato's class in the late summer of 1970. The musical group, Bread, topped the Billboard pop chart just before Labor Day with the song, *Make It With You*. NBC's hit comedy series *The Mary Tyler Moore* show was about to debut and begin its unprecedented eight-year season. Our class was still together, a summer wiser, with a sense of adventure waiting on the other side of winter as we concluded our tenure at Mt. Pleasant Elementary School.

Sixth grade was a flash in the pan. I can remember going into Mr. DePrato's room on the Wednesday after Labor Day in 1970 and seeing him stand in front of the class on the day before the school year ended on a warm and sunny June day in 1971 telling the entire class that we were all graduating to junior high school. It was truly our first sense of reaching a special milestone with exciting adventure ahead.

But all of us would not be moving to the same junior high school. With two junior high schools the same distance from Mt. Pleasant some of us would go northeast to Normandin Junior High and some of us would head south to Keith Junior High. There seemed to be a dimension of melancholy that none of us could put our arms around or express well but when it came down to the dismissal bell for the last time at Mt. Pleasant, the prevailing spirit was one of the unspeakable adventure of moving on to the next chapter. The warm sun greeted us as we walked home dreaming of the beach, ice cream at Friendly's, and late night fireworks for the Fourth of July.

Chapter 2
Probability 100%

With junior high and high school now approaching, only a handful of people that I knew believed that my career path had been set. The cement was poured early and by this time it was beginning to cure to the point where making any kind of other career impression was next to impossible. Just ask anyone who was very close to me at the time: my parents, siblings, Jim Buckley and one other very special uncle.

Uncle Arthur

Arthur Langlois married my father's sister, Irene. My grandfather Damase owned farm property between New Bedford and Lakeville and had my father work the farm at a very young age. It was mainly an egg and chicken farm. The work was arduous but had its advantages. Nonetheless, it was not the kind of work for which my father had a passion so he had no long-term interest in the farm at all. After Arthur married Irene, he agreed to purchase the farm and to make it his livelihood.

My earliest recollections of Uncle Arthur and Aunt Irene was when he remodeled and expanded the house on the farm. In order to get there, you had to travel down a half-mile long dirt road well away from the main road. The farm itself was well landscaped with small rolling hills filled with a vibrant green lawn. Their house stood on the top of the largest hill and overlooked the farm with the chicken coop about a hundred yards to the north.

My father used to love to tell stories about how there was no electricity running to the house back when he manned it in the 1930s and how dark it got after sundown. Earlier in the evening my father had stumbled upon some foxfire, a type of fungus that emits light much like the chemical light from a firefly. Fascinated by the bright glowing clumps, he collected a large handful and brought them back to the farmhouse and placed them on the wood floor before he grew tired and turned in for the night.

My grandfather intended to pay him a visit that night to see how everything was going. When he entered the dark house, all he saw was a scattering of what he thought were glowing embers on a wood floor. Without delay, he began stomping on the foxfire in hopes to snuff it out. Instead, the foxfire grew more luminescent as it crushed under his feet while spreading quickly throughout the room. My father was awakened to the sounds of someone stomping their feet like a mad man. He quickly found out that it was his father trying to extinguish embers that were as cold as the floor on which they were spreading.

That farmhouse had come a long way since the 1930s. By the time my brother and I were born, it was a stunning house-on-a-hill, beautifully decorated and filled with my uncle and aunt's distinctive and joyful laugh. They were childless but loved my brother and me as if we were their sons. We later found out that my parents had entrusted them as our guardians in their will if anything ever happened to them. While we are all grateful that the option was never needed, it was a wonderful choice.

While the majority of his living was made in the egg farming business, he also loved gardening. Living on a farm gave him all the room in the world to design and maintain any kind of garden that he could conjure up in his mind. Every year we marveled over his meticulous garden. The produce that came from it had a dimension that grocery store produce aisles would never contain. After all, it was fresh and organic. The corn was never more than minutes from the garden to the pot of boiling water. The tomatoes were still warm from the sun by the time they were sliced on our plates for dinner. Everyone should have that experience at least once in their lives.

Being the farmer that he was, weather was always important to him. Like me, Uncle Arthur was familiar with every television meteorologist in both the Providence and Boston markets and he had his favorites, most of whom were mine as well.

Countless times our families sat around his living room for a visit. In the cool months, scents of wood burning permeated the place as he always had an inviting fire going in the fireplace. As the wood popped and mixed with the sounds of conversation, invariably Uncle Arthur and I would talk about the weather for hours on end. It was a monopoly on the conversation that went far deeper than surface "weather talk." We talked about long-term patterns, weather theory, and took apart specific weather phenomenon. He would often raise his eyebrows in surprise when I elaborated on something he had never heard before.

Uncle Arthur's favorite weather instrument, a beautiful, sleek and modern German-made barometer, prominently and faithfully informed him of impending weather changes before the 6 o'clock weathercasts. The barometer was a special-order item for which my aunt saved a long time so it had a special meaning well beyond being one of the most sensitive barometers I had ever seen. Invariably, he and I would always walk over to check the air pressure at least a couple of times with every visit, talking about the implications of what we observed.

Decades later I was asked if there was anything that I wished to inherit after their passing. I asked that if they had no plans for his barometer I would love to find a special place for it in our home. They were delighted with my request.

Not long after, first my Uncle Arthur then my Aunt Irene passed away. In the chaos that followed that difficult time period, the barometer that had such special meaning to me vanished. No one seemed to know what happened to it. While no one could ever take away the investments of time and love they gave to my brother and me, I was still disappointed that the token of the mutual passion that Uncle Arthur and I shared would not hang on my wall.

Some years later I surfed eBay to see what kinds of barometers people were selling. There were literally hundreds for sale. I looked at each one. Near the end of the listing my eyes snapped to one of the thumbnail images on the bottom. It looked like my Uncle Arthur's barometer. After opening that particular auction and taking a closer look, there it was. I was convinced it was his barometer. The seller lived in Michigan and I was naturally curious where he had acquired it. After repeated emails asking him about the particulars I received no response whatsoever. Not wanting to let it go, I made a bid that no one could match. I did win the auction and a week later received the barometer, safe and sound and working like it did when it was hanging on their wall. Events like that make me marvel even more than pondering the parting of the Red Sea for the Israelites. We serve a God who is interested right down to the very details of our lives and can easily arrange a phenomenal event like that.

To this very day memories of cozy evenings at their farmhouse flood my mind every time our family starts a fire in the fireplace. There is something about the smell of wood burning and the sound of the sap popping that will forever bring my Uncle Arthur's familiar chuckle into my ears as if he was sitting right next to me.

Mr. Peters

After spending four years at Mt.Pleasant Elementary, Normandin Junior High was quite a change. It was considerably larger and much farther away. I could no longer walk to school with my brother. Instead, I took the bus at the corner of Sutton and Highland within eyeshot of our front door and the front door of Mt. Pleasant at just before 7 o'clock. The earlier bus call didn't really sink in until winter when the group waiting for the bus often huddled together in the pre-dawn darkness, wind-whipped by rain and snow.

Mornings tended to be boring affairs waiting outside the school for the bell to ring, announcing to all of us that it was time to head for homeroom. That all changed after having a music teacher by the name of Mr. Peters.

Mr. Peters was unique. Always energetic, and peculiarly articulate in his speech, he commanded respect from his students from the moment they entered the door, despite his somewhat gangly frame whose large bald spot drew attention to his egg-shaped head. His form was deceiving in that students thought they could get away with much more than he allowed. But he was tough and required much of everyone because he genuinely cared for each student that walked through his large third-floor music room.

He introduced us to a fun little instrument known as the melodica, an instrument made popular by jazz and reggae musicians in the late 1960s. I took to it like a duck to water and Mr. Peters noticed my unusual interest. Shortly after, he asked if I would consider coming in before homeroom period in the morning to mentor a group of handpicked students and to teach them how to play. At first I was intimidated by the implications. How would these other students react to being taught how to play an instrument from another student? Mr. Peters insisted that I had a gift and that I needed to share it with others. I accepted the challenge. Every morning before the homeroom bell rang, I met with a group of six others for fifteen minutes. While he monitored me from a distance, Mr. Peters rarely interfered with the tutoring sessions, and only occasionally would he privately make a few suggestions on how to draw the best out of them.

I can't remember what the end goal of the tutoring session was, but I do clearly remember what it did to my confidence as an individual. In hindsight, I now wonder if Mr. Peters actually saw a dormant part of me that needed a catalyst to energize it. The task also kept me busy in what could have become an unproductive idle time. Mr. Peters knew all too well that students with too much idle time on their hands sometimes used it to their own disadvantage.

After junior high school ended, our paths diverged and they never rejoined, but somehow I think he knows just how important those few miles of his walking alongside me turned out to be.

"Aunty" Alice Hargraves

Ask any junior high school student what his or her favorite period was and you will invariably hear the response - "Lunch." It was something we all anticipated daily. Every week, my mother would clip out the menu from the New Bedford *Standard-Times* and post it on the fridge with one of many magnets that adorned it. It was not an exercise in futility since both my brother and I would check the menu board before preparing to leave for school. Most of the time, we approved of the day's choice. Every once in a while, one or both of us would groan. Mystery meat anyone?

Initially, I brown-bagged my lunch from home for a little while until I started getting peanut butter and jelly sandwiches with a slice of American cheese on it. Out of obligation I tried it, but soon would give away the slice of cheese to someone else who liked cheese more than I did at the time. The convenience of buying lunch at school was more appealing anyway.

Mom suggested that I look into the student lunch work program. She was familiar with it since she had started working part-time in the New Bedford public school system as a cafeteria worker. Students helped the paid workers usually in the dishwashing room in exchange for a full meal at the beginning of the lunch period. Not only did I get my daily hot meal free, it was one less thing I had to carry to school. Mom liked it because she knew I was getting a good lunch with the benefit of developing a healthy work ethic.

The two paid workers in the dishwashing room were Alice and Sofie. The two silver-haired ladies, who were both somewhere in their sixties, were also the best of friends and relied on each other to maintain joy through the sometimes crazy-paced lunch periods. They also cared very deeply for the students who worked with them. Alice couldn't stand our calling her "Mrs. Hargraves," yet "Alice" was far too informal and disrespectful. She insisted that we all simply call her, "Aunty." It was very fitting.

There were two lunch tray return windows at Normandin that split the difference between two cafeterias of equal size. Aunty was always working on the north side and Sofie next to her on the south window. Despite my always having lunch in the south wing, somehow I started working daily with Aunty on the north side. Once I got to know Aunty well, I had no desire to work any other position even though it was the messiest job. We scraped the leftover food from the incoming dishes into a barrel and stacked the dishes and silverware into special racks that were slowly pulled through the commercial dishwasher. Another couple of student workers were waiting for the hot, steamy racks from which they took the clean and hot dishes and placed them on carts to be transported back to the cafeteria line.

As we were working, Aunty would always want to hear about every detail of our day both in and out of school. Like a surrogate Mom, she always encouraged us to study hard and strive academically. Invariably, she would ask what I thought the weather would do in the next few days. On Fridays, she would often quietly call me over and covertly place a dime in my hand and close it.

"Go buy an ice cream sandwich. My treat. We've had a long and hard week."

Then she would shoo me quietly out to the cafeteria so that the others would not see that she had given favor to one of her student workers. Coming back with an ice cream sandwich in my belly, Aunty would wink and place her finger over her lips as we began the task of cleaning the dishes and preparing the silverware for the dishwasher.

Some days were easier than others. Fish stick days were pretty easy. Meatloaf with mashed potatoes and brown gravy was a different story. I enjoyed that lunch but knew full well that a messy fifteen minutes was waiting for us. On occasion, the trays came fast and furious and it usually was on the days we had messier meals. We would speed up with robotic precision almost to the point of looking like we had consumed a pot of coffee each. Just about when it was too much to handle and tempers were flaring at the students flinging their half-eaten meals at us, Aunty would grab my hands to tell me to stop. Not wanting any of us to succumb to irritated tempers, she saw the humor in our maniacal pace and started to laugh. In a single moment she defused a dishwashing room time bomb with her joyful humor. It happened more times in any given year than I have fingers and toes. That paradigm shift made a mundane and messy job into a merry and memorable one.

Normandin Junior High was only a two-year stop for us since the brand new high school was ready for the ninth grade freshman class in the autumn of 1973. Since my brother, Denié, was two years younger than me, he started attending Normandin when I became a freshman in the brand-new high school that opened on Hathaway Boulevard in 1973. His two-year tenure with Aunty was equally special in many of the same ways.

Mary Barney

I was happy to watch my mother get involved in cafeteria work in the New Bedford public school system. She enjoyed being around people, loved children of all ages, and the food service seemed to be a passion of hers adopted from my father's profession as a chef and restaurant operator. While she would readily admit that her employment was to secure additional medical benefits for all of us, her work was a source of joy.

She made friends easily with those with whom she worked. Many of her friends were of the lifelong variety and stayed in touch with her well past the time she retired from her work in a number of cafeterias. Each was special in her own way, but one stood out from the crowd.

Mary was very likely one of Mom's closest friends in life's journey. Maybe it was because of Mary's refreshing honesty. She was always unapologetically honest, but always with a kind of "joie de vivre." It was so enchanting that she could tell you that your breath smelled like the Acushnet River at low tide and you would chuckle and genuinely thank her for it. At times, Mom needed that no-nonsense perspective, and she knew it.

As far as we were able to tell, Mary did not have to work. Her husband, Stan, was a well respected business man who did well in his career. She worked because she enjoyed being around others. The paycheck was an unnecessary bonus, much of which she gave to others.

I cannot count the number of times when she would pop in for a visit and while Mom ran into another room to get something, Mary would motion me over and quietly stuff a crisp twenty dollar bill in my hand, telling me to be quiet with her mischievous smile. She was caught by Mom perhaps only once or twice in the act. Years later we told her that she must have done that dozens of times while my brother and I were in high school and college.

In the summer of 1979 after my sophomore year at Lyndon

State College in Vermont, I made plans to visit the girl whose beautiful blue eyes captured my heart. Sally was from Ohio and an invitation to come to her house during summer break for a visit was all I needed. Wanting to be frugal with the money I earned from McDonald's, I opted to take the train from Boston to Cleveland instead of flying. Getting to and from the Amtrak train station in Framingham, Massachusetts, was going to be a trick. Dad worked at the Orchid Diner during the day, and Mom wasn't real thrilled about driving anywhere near Boston for anything.

Knowing how nervous my mother was about driving anywhere outside New Bedford into unfamiliar surroundings, Mary volunteered to play the part of chauffeur for the two-hour round trip to get me to the train station and to pick me up when I returned as well. She also served up pearls of wisdom to a mother who was unsettled about a girl she knew very little about and with whom she had not played cupid (something she had tried in vain to do on a number of occasions). Mary reminded my mother that she had invested good values into her children and that she needed to give us the room to spread our wings.

"I want to hear some clicks," was Mary's famous rhetoric before putting any vehicle in gear that she drove. Well before mandatory seat belt laws were enacted, her public relations pitch for maximizing safety formed a deep river of thought whose water still flows to this day every time I reach for my shoulder harness. I think I have told this story to my son, Noah, more than a few dozen times, usually when we are buckling in to go somewhere together.

Mom's friendship with Mary went deep, but it was far too short. Not long after I graduated from college, Mary's heart condition caused her to unexpectedly depart for eternity with a breathy call from her bedroom to Stan, who was watching television in their living room. When he walked into the room to find out what she calling out for, he realized that Mary was saying her goodbye. She was gone.

Mom has always been a very strong individual, having weathered many difficult trials and tribulations over her entire lifetime, but this event took the wind out of Mom's sail for quite some time. Like a sailboat caught in the doldrums she pressed on as best she could and continued life's journey without her friend while waiting for a fresh breeze to bring life back up to speed.

Even today I think often of Mary. The wisdom, honesty and generosity that she not only modeled but lived out daily was one more steadfast compass that was given to me for the road ahead.

George Kropp

I grew up in what I would call a typical middle-class American family. Many things shaped our lives, but those things that were given most weight were faith, family and education.

Faith was an important dimension for all of us. At an early age, it was my mother who showed me how to pray. Together, our family attended church every week without fail. My father often said that it was one of the places that brought him the most peace. My brother and I also enjoyed getting plugged into church activities and helping where we were able. There was something satisfying about serving in the house of God. Yet there was something that seemed to be missing. I could not identify it, point my finger at it, or even point myself in a direction that might help me find whatever it was that was missing. Because this intuition was so vague, I did not give it much thought. I went on with the business of being a adolescent and growing up. If I found this missing piece of life's jigsaw puzzle it would be a wonderful bonus. If I didn't, no big issue. I wasn't going to lose any sleep over it since I had the big picture and could operate just fine with that.

My sister, Henriette, lived at the bottom of Sawyer Street only a ten-minute walk away from our house. Being a divorced, single mother of two daughters, my brother and I would frequently visit her to break up the monotony of her day and sometimes ours.

She had a number of casual friends that we came to know. One of them would change the course of my life.

George Kropp was an older gentleman who showed kindness to my sister in many ways. Their paths first crossed at the snack bar at a local merchandise shop on the avenue only two blocks from where Henriette lived. George had the kind of laugh that was gravelly and full while his belly and shoulders shook with delight. My brother Denié and I would find ways to make him laugh, because when he laughed we couldn't help but to do the same. There was something about his personality that can be described only as pure joy even though George was just an ordinary kind of fellow. How can a joy like that be real? What was driving this guy's boat?

While there was no romantic undercurrent at all between George and my sister, he went out of his way to befriend our family and would sometimes even accept my parent's invitation to stay for something to eat.

One sunny, early summer Sunday, George accompanied my sister and my two nieces to our house for an after-church lunch. George was in his Sunday duds and my brother and I quickly went to work on him trying to make him laugh, an easy task.

After a wonderful lunch in the backyard and after the long laughs and funny stories had settled down, George had something special to share. As we all sat around in a circle on summer lawn chairs in the shade of our mammoth sixty-foot pine tree, George drew us all in with telling us the story of Christ's rescue mission on Earth. It's a story I had heard time and time again, but this time it was told in a way that made the story come to life. I began to see that this ancient event from two thousand years ago had personal implications on my life today and that this event required a personal response.

George went on to explain that what Christ brought was a very expensive gift given freely to us. But this gift would cost Him dearly - His very life on the cross. He paid our sin debt in full. This gift had to be claimed in person and by faith. We could not earn our way into heaven. We could not say enough "Our Fathers" to grant us entrance into heaven. Just going to church every week does not make you a true Christian, in the same way that being born in a garage does not automatically make you a car. You had to approach Christ by faith to receive this amazing gift, realizing that you could bring nothing to Him except your own soul to redeem.

George was not trying to sell us "his religion." He was trying to share the gift he himself received by faith. As I sat and listened with great interest, my mother became defensive and told George that while he was welcome anytime, he could "keep his religion" since we had ours. I was a bit embarrassed but not surprised. While the rest of the conversation was cordial, it was noticeably cooler until it ended in George's departure.

George may have thought that he had failed in his attempt to share the Gospel with us, but he was faithful in planting the seed in my soul. I considered the missing piece of the puzzle at the center of it. The longer I chewed on it the clearer it became that this was the missing piece I had hoped to find. To solidify it, I began reading the Bible that my sister had given to me. As I read the Gospel of John and then the other Gospels it dawned on me that while I believed *in* Christ, I did not know Him personally as my Savior, my Rescuer, my Redeemer... *my* Lord. One night as I lay in bed waiting to fall asleep and considering all these insights, I prayed a simple prayer and invited Christ to indwell my heart and soul. There were no fireworks. There was no lightning and thunder from heaven. Just a high school kid who realized that this missing piece was the most important part of life's puzzle.

Because George took the time to share the greatest news of all, he started a chain reaction of events of which he would be unaware on this side of eternity. After engaging my father in countless and seemingly fruitless conversations about the need for each person to receive Christ's gift, I witnessed my father come to an understanding of the Gospel several months before he died. Many other family members, friends, co-workers and acquaintances came to the same personal decision. It was never by winning a theological debate. It was through showing everyone love and respect and by living life in front of the people in my sphere with the kind of honor and integrity that Christ calls every one of His followers to live. Only then will someone listen to what you want to share because they now want what you have, that is a relationship with Christ.

I understood this to an even deeper level one Sunday when I heard an aged Monsignor Bérubé deliver the Sunday morning message as guest speaker at Sacred Heart Church. He told us that he was once troubled by a passage of Scripture that he did not understand and asked the Lord to help him grasp it. He paused. You could hear only the humming of the heating system as everyone waited for his next sentence.

"You know," he slowly said with a peaceful smile, "Jesus spoke to me plainly." He then told the captivated congregation how Christ cleared his vision by asking him a rhetorical question. He spoke of his conversation with the Lord as if He was his best friend and sharing one-on-one. Christ was always a wonderful but seemingly distant Savior to me, but the Monsignor delivered a paradigm shift that made an indelible impression. The Jesus of the Gospel is always closer than we think if only we dare have the faith to approach Him not only as Savior and Redeemer, but as a true Friend.

One of the strangest things about sharing the Gospel is that the more you give that gift to others (especially those who receive it), the more you experience that gift yourself. I now understand why George Kropp was such a joyful person who didn't give a second thought to making a detour in his own journey in order to share a special gift.

Rodney Cejka

One of my favorite poets, Robert Frost, once said, "Do not follow where the path may lead. Go instead where there is no path and leave a trail." And leaving a trail was something I was unconsciously doing since there was no path to where I wanted to go. Finding the path of least resistance was half the fun.

After almost a year or so of riding the local weekend airwaves at WBSM and being accepted as a reliable fixture and as "one of the guys," I received a letter from another student of weather who lived in Fairhaven, one town east of New Bedford. Mike Cejka was also in the graduating class of 1977 and equally passionate about weather. We became fast friends, exchanging ideas and resources and talking about weather at a peer level that left others looking at us as if we were speaking a foreign language.

Since the radio station's transmitter and studios were on Pope's Island in New Bedford Harbor, right on the New Bedford-Fairhaven line, I would often ride my bike down to Mike's home to see his elaborate weather-gathering bunker in his basement. I related to his passion for gathering the freshest data in any manner possible. Mike had an old teletype machine that he rigged up to decode shortwave packet radio signals that carried surface weather observations. Mike had to be one of the most resourceful people I had ever run into. It was easy to see why after meeting his father and mother, both strong encouraging forces in his life.

Mr. Cejka (Rodney, or "Rod" as he is referred to by his family and friends) immediately received me as a special friend to his son. He made me feel like I was an adopted son from the get-go.

During the winter of our junior year, Mike and his father invited me to join them on one of their weekend trips to hit the slopes at King Ridge Ski Area in New Hampshire. Having never done any skiing in my life, while excited to go, I was a bit apprehensive about going down a snow-covered mountain with two boards on my feet, two boards that do not have any brakes. Yet the thought of skiing had always appealed to me since I loved anything associated with snow.

The Friday afternoon school bell rang and all I could think about was the weekend of snowy slopes and mountains. A few hours later the skies were losing all dusk as we drove northbound on I-93 in Mr. Cejka's station wagon, feeling the air growing colder with every passing mile. While Mike's father preferred classical music, he tuned in to one of the pop stations for us. The scent of his pipe tobacco was smooth and sweet as Gary Wright's 1976 title track, "Dream Weaver," peppered the airwaves. We settled into a hotel room in Concord on Friday night. My first ski adventure would begin Saturday morning.

That weekend was likely the most memorable of my junior year in high school. Both Mike and Mike's father showed me great grace and patience as they taught me how to ski. Despite continually falling and getting physically wiped out trying to keep my balance, I was hooked. Between their gifted instruction and my stalwart determination, by Sunday I was gliding down the slopes with much more finesse. Only once did I fall, and I'm embarrassed to admit that it was while I was standing in a lift line.

Mike and his father were instrumental in starting a lifelong enjoyment of a sport that I still enjoy today. Two winters ago I had the joy of introducing my young son to skiing. There isn't a single trip we have taken that I have not thought about that winter weekend in 1976.

Mr. Cejka had another gift that he gave me throughout my college years. Since Mike became my roommate during my sophomore and junior years, I would have the opportunity to see Mike's parents whenever they came up to the college for a visit. With my father and mother not able to make the four-hour trek as easily, Mr. Cejka filled in the gap and became a proxy father to me. He looked for every opportunity to include me in their family's itinerary if I was available. He was also not shy about encouraging Mike and all of his friends with the kind of manly physical affirmation that every father should learn how to give his sons. I knew full well that my father loved my siblings and me deeply, but we never saw him express it well until the last few years of his life. He was considerably older and from a different era whose men were taught to be quiet and stately. Mr. Cejka stood in that temporary gap at a critical season in my life as I slowly sailed from the often turbulent waters of adolescence to an uncertain ocean of adulthood.

Decades later, when my father died, I received the biggest gift to my grieving spirit when I saw Mr. Cejka arrive at the wake to pay his respects and to support me and my family. He was battling his own physical challenges at the time which made his visit that much more meaningful.

Watching both Mike and his father live their lives has been better than any Sunday message about living a Christ-like life. They were a living example of how to operate in the Christian virtues. I was amazed to see Mike apply a preternatural grace to situations, even toward me, where grace was not only unearned but unwarranted. They never had to talk the talk. They walked the walk and invariably went the extra mile.

Charlie Taylor

For a time, New Bedford was fortunate to have one of the three network television affiliates in the city. New Bedford actually belonged to the larger Providence market from which the other two affiliates operated. The studios of WTEV (now WLNE) were located only a few miles away on County Street in the downtown district. I vaguely remember the buzz in New Bedford when the station went on the air. I was almost four years old. As our black and white television slowly warmed up, we saw a test pattern on New Year's morning in 1963. New Bedford had its own television station and an ABC affiliate to boot.

In the 1970s, Charlie Taylor was the chief meteorologist. Charlie was a tall, thin and quiet man with a gentle smile. Our paths crossed when I joined the Explorer's club that had a local broadcast focus. The formation of the club met with some success initially. Our group helped to write and conceptualize a local promo about the Explorer's Club. Ben Schneider, who worked at WTEV as general talent and occasional weather fill-in, was our club's host. He took us through the process of preparing the promo that we would eventually tape, shoot and edit. If good enough, it might even be aired. Unfortunately, the process ground to a halt when he broke the news to us that the local unions would not allow the club to touch any of the equipment. Without the ability to see a realized project after working for months to come up with it, the club members began slowly losing interest. Only a weekend camp outing with Ben at the end of the school year held us together as a group. The Explorer chapter disappeared over the summer, but my visits continued.

In much the same fashion as I did with WBSM, I managed to befriend not only Charlie Taylor, but also Ben, news director Truman Taylor (no relation to Charlie), the art department director, many of the engineers and the lobby receptionist.

My interest in their work over a long time genuinely fascinated me and that allowed them to extend a great favor to me. This favor meant that I did not need to "sign in" as a visitor when coming to shadow Charlie. All of the film engineers knew me by name since some of the station's weather equipment was located in the same room as all of the film chains. Having free reign of the teletype room and main studio, I would lay out all the information that I knew Charlie liked to look at when he came in. After a while, I would actually design a forecast and walk to the main studio to use the magnetic letters to prepare the forecast. On occasion, Charlie liked what I had prepared and left it completely as was.

What a thrill to ride back home and to see my leg work for Charlie actually on television. The rush of adrenalin of seeing something I helped to make kept me coming back for more.

Once again, the extraordinary kindness of a professional willing to mentor a weather-crazy kid who was young enough to be his son propelled me several steps closer to the stars for which I was aiming.

Charlie eventually left WTEV for Louisville, Kentucky where he enjoyed a long running popularity. A few years ago, I was stunned to read Charlie's obituary in a professional journal. While he was ten or fifteen years my senior, that was still too young. Wanting to somehow honor him, I dedicated one of my weathercasts to him by way of giving him a public "thank you," one which my soul believed he somehow received through the curtain of eternity.

The Staff At WBSM

Ever since I can remember, I loved listening to the radio. My earliest recollections include a couple of tabletop and portable models that were AM only. FM was still somewhat experimental and still under the radar of most households but was soon to emerge. Until then, my brother and I would often sit on our front porch in the summer afternoons listening to top-40 radio on our two favorite radio stations back then, WPRO in Providence and WRKO in Boston. As summer afternoon thunderstorms approached, we would play on the porch and watch as the sky grew darker, and wait for the thunderstorm to arrive to cool us off from the stuffy heat. All the while, some of our favorite songs from the late 60s and early 70s had to compete with the loud crackles of static from the lightning discharges. To this day, whenever I hear any of these songs on stations playing what are now oldies, they don't quite sound right without the crackling noises that dominated AM radio whenever there were nearby thunderstorms.

While WPRO and WRKO were the favorites of the younger generation, our home was dominated by the local station, 1420 WBSM. Every morning, we would wake to the kitchen radio blasting out local news from Jim Phillips and live weather updates from meteorologist John Parisi who lived in Hyannis. Then there was the local fish market update, a ten-minute report identifying the vessels and their catch in pounds and the price paid for them at the New Bedford dock. It was hosted by WBSM fixture, Bill Brennan, who racked up over thirty years as the "Voice of the Waterfront." Add some occasional music and a popular three-hour call-in program between 9 AM and noon called "Open Line," hosted by Stan Lipp, and you get some of the best local radio that was ever broadcast.

I would often pretend to be a radio disc jockey with the record player in our bedroom, reading news teletype copy for the top-of-the-hour newscast along with weather updates. When I wasn't pretending, I was learning by listening to the local disc jockeys and newscasters. From time to time I would actually call into the radio talk show, "Open Line," to voice my young opinion about whatever topic they were tackling. Being a guest on "Open Line" was my debut in broadcasting. That was probably in the early 1970s. Once I tasted what that was like, I wanted to do more than just be a guest caller on a local radio talk show. I wanted to be the youngest radio weathercaster in the country. Trying to figure out how to navigate to that goal was my biggest obstacle but I did not let that discourage me in any way. I was going to do it somehow.

Dick Stevens

In the summer of 1974, I began visiting WBSM on a regular basis. Just being in the environment allowed me to absorb and learn a great deal about how a radio station worked. Dick Stevens was the weekend afternoon program host at the time and we developed a rapport as I watched him prepare for newscasts, cue records to the beginning of songs on the turntables, and prepare to read live commercial copy. In the course of conversation, I let him know that my real passion was weather forecasting and broadcasting, and that I would love to do that on his program. In a bold moment, I asked him if I could. He leaned back in his chair smoking a large, light-brown cigar and looked up toward the ceiling for a moment, then smiled.

"I'll tell you what I will do," Dick thoughtfully replied.

"How would you like to do a beach report? You know, water temperatures, times of high tide and some of the wind reports at area beaches. Would you like to try that?"

I jumped at the chance without thought. Perhaps Dick thought that I would try it once and that my visits would stop. But that first Saturday afternoon "boat and beach" report that I did in July of 1974 was one step closer to my goal. Like clockwork I showed up every weekend afternoon to prepare and deliver a thirty-second "boat and beach" report on live radio during the Dick Stevens program. I sensed that Dick had a new respect for this fifteen year old who was punctual and persistent.

July waned and the August back-to-school sales were in high gear. I was ready for my sophomore year but I was not ready to see summer weather disappear. That meant that Dick would no longer have the need for a "boat and beach" report. But after Labor Day weekend, I persisted in my visits and asked if I could provide short weekend forecasts since John Parisi only provided forecasts during the weekday. I found favor in the eyes of the staff, including then general manager, Bob Nims, who agreed to shift me from my weekend afternoon cameos to weekend mornings, providing a short thirty-second forecast for the morning newscasts then anchored by Jim Phillips.

On Saturday, September 14, 1974, I rose early and rode my bike down to the WBSM studio on Pope's Island in New Bedford harbor by 6:30 A.M. and filed my first weekend forecast. Jim was there to show me how to record them on audio carts so that he could play them during his newscasts and he always left me the option of filing my forecasts by phone from home (as John Parisi did daily) or to come in to record them at the station. As long as the weather was not severely prohibitive, I preferred to surround myself with the ambiance of the radio station and to learn as much as I could from all the people around me. Until I could get my driver's license, I peddled my way to Pope's Island in everything from muggy heat or brutal wind chills to stunning sunshine or driving rain. Having snow on the road was the only thing that forced me to call in the weather segments. The years of peddling several miles eventually became my preferred mode of transportation as long as the weather co-operated even after I received my license. It was not only a great way to get exercise, but the eventual result was that my legs grew strong by default. By the time I started college, I was able to leg press over a thousand pounds cleanly.

Jim Phillips

While it was Dick Stevens that opened a crack in the door for me to begin my broadcast career, many others at WBSM came alongside and mentored me with an abundance of patience.

Jim Phillips was (and still is) the voice of WBSM news and he genuinely liked giving me the responsibility of updating the recorded call-in weather line and having a weather cart ready to play for his newscasts. Those were two fewer things for which he had to make time. He graciously gave me free reign of the newsroom as I ripped and sorted teletype news copy looking for anything weather related.

He was not only good at his craft, but loved sharing helpful tips for people who had a passion for broadcasting. It was Jim that introduced me to the three-finger, newsroom style of typing that would send any typing teacher into a fit. But in a world in which you needed to press the manual typewriter keys hard enough to make seven carbon copies, the pinky was worthless. Since I never took typing class in any formal setting, the three-finger method is the one I still use today with considerable speed and proficiency.

Jim also taught me the art of time management. This was not by sage advice or lecture but by simple observation. The clock never stopped if he fell behind. The newscast would be ready at the top of every hour no matter what broke his routine. There were plenty of those moments in a heavy news day. Watching him juggle it all was like watching a maestro conduct a complex symphony. In a business that is filled with the pressure of deadlines, I never once saw him lose his composure.

Stan Lipp

Stan Lipp was another staple name of WBSM for decades. He was host of the ever popular call-in program, "Open Line," on which I made my radio debut as a youthful caller. The program aired Monday through Saturday, so I was able to see Stan every Saturday morning as I recorded my forecasts.

Stan recently retired from "Open Line," and I was thrilled to have participated in an audio vignette sendoff during his final week on the air. In it, I recalled one event when I stepped into the news booth to record the forecast cart before heading home. I could see Stan's program going on live in the next studio through the soundproof glass. The news booth's sound board was fairly easy to operate but I did not check one very important switch. It was the switch that took the board off line. Sitting down and putting a new tape cart in the machine, I turned the microphone on, checked the levels, and started recording the forecast. Little did I know that I was going out live and stepping all over Stan's program. Stan tried to get my attention but I thought he was giving me a friendly wave. Not until Jim zipped through the door and flicked the master switch off did I realize what had just happened. A rush of adrenalin flooded my body and I went numb thinking that I had just made my last forecast. I had just interrupted the dean of New Bedford's talk show airwaves. Shaken and embarrassed, I wanted to run out and never return. It was an egregious broadcast error but Stan's grace rose to a level I had never experienced from anyone.

Proverbs 12:25 says that "An anxious heart weighs a man down, but a kind word cheers him up." Stan would have been justified to have given me a strong rebuke at the very least, but as I went in to ask for his forgiveness during a break in the program, his kind and patient words covered the offense. It was an extra mile of grace that I will never forget.

Jim Loomis

Jim Loomis was another disc jockey whose sunny disposition was contagious. He wore a distinguished beard and mustache that framed his smile that was a bright, luminescent white. His walk was unmistakable. With a specially carved cane, he calculated his way through the station with slow, labored steps, one hip being more helpful than the other. Even with a physical challenge such as his, Jim never once complained about anything. His joy was a striking contrast.

There were many times during his shift when I would run back to the station's old-fashioned bottle pop machine right behind studio A near the transmitter room and grab a thirty-five cent bottle of a new pop to which I was introduced from this machine. With my fix of Mountain Dew in hand, I would return to studio A and shoot the breeze with Jim.

Jim was quite a witty wordsmith. During one of our chat sessions during his Sunday on-air shift he looked at me as I slurped another "Dew," smiled, and said, "We have a name for your kind in this business. You are a meteorological prognosticatorial engineer!"

The phrase stuck. I humbly added "associate." Every once in a while during his on-air shift, he would introduce the weather segments with the lengthy title. It was delivered with a touch of tongue-in-cheek, but with the kind of respect that made his intro to my segment endearing.

Bill Brennan

Bill Brennan, the "Voice of the Waterfront," was another WBSM staffer who took a special interest in encouraging me in my pursuit of a career in broadcast meteorology. Being someone who was close to the fishing industry, Bill understood the importance of weather and its impact on the vessels out on Georges Bank and Nantucket Shoals and beyond. With his captivating story-telling style, he shared many stories of how a weather forecast could mean safely navigating home with your catch of the day or losing a ship with its crew when caught in the kinds of storms we saw depicted in the film, "The Perfect Storm."

One day, he came into the station with several books on nautical weather. They were considered classics and out of print, yet he loaned them to me for as long as I liked to peruse them.

Because of his relationship with the U.S. Coast Guard, it was Bill who insisted that I should be considered to teach a short course on meteorology at one of their summer academies at Fort Taber. I was nervous about accepting the challenge, but Bill assured me that my weather knowledge was far more advanced than those attending the seminar and that he had faith in my ability to bring the subject to life. He helped me find the confidence that I needed to accept a teaching task that forced me to stretch my own knowledge.

The Final Week

Three years had passed. I graduated from high school and took on a summer job as the weekday morning opener for the McDonald's on King's Highway to help pay for some of my college expenses. On weekends, like clockwork, I made my morning run to

WBSM. My three-year run was about to conclude. In the broadcast business, continuity is important. I realized that with a nine-month period of absence during the most active weather seasons, returning for only three months at a time would be next to impossible.

My last weekend there should have been August 27-28, 1977. But Bob Nims, then station manager, approached me with a proposition. Long-time weekday meteorologist John Parisi was taking a weeklong vacation beginning September 5th. He asked if I'd be interested in filling in for John, something Bob had never before asked me to do. Not knowing when I would return to any airwaves with a regular gig, I jumped at the chance, not knowing exactly how I would accomplish this from a college campus over two hundred miles away.

Without the luxuries of still non-existent pre-paid phone cards, cheap long-distance and internet audio streams, the weather feeds by ordinary telephone went well on Monday and Tuesday. But on that Wednesday, the first day of class, something happened. Arriving at the college weather lab at 5:00 AM in a fog that was as thick as chicken gumbo, the door was locked. As I checked all of the possible entrances, I had that sinking feeling. All efforts to contact the station failed. It wasn't until much later that I was able to call the station to let them know what happened. In the meantime, back in New Bedford, a worried mother's imagination went into hyper-drive imagining the worst since she did not hear me that morning.

Fortunately, the final two days went smoothly and I sang my WBSM swan song on the morning of September 9, 1977. Not having the time to linger in the afterglow, it was time to move ahead, but not without a rich library of knowledge and encouragement from a radio family that taught me how to catch a wave and ride it.

Chapter 3

The Great Adventure

It has been over thirty years since one of my fondest adventures began. I think it's best captured in excepts from an email that I sent to my brother Denié, remembering the events from that weekend. It was such a special and exciting time that I can vividly recall details that would have faded in most people's memories decades ago:

Saturday, September 3, 1977

After a long day of packing the day before and only on a few hours of sleep, we were all up before five and by six we were on the road. It was still warm, muggy and mostly cloudy. Anticipating some rain, we covered the roof rack with plastic and left it there just in case we ran into rain.

We did run into darker clouds and rain showers in southern New Hampshire. We were all glad the plastic was there. Suddenly, we broke out into brilliant sunshine in Plymouth, NH and it was stunning! Sunny, beautiful, crisp, deep blue skies, puffy clouds. It looked like heaven. We arrived in Lyndonville on a beautiful late morning.

You could see Burke Mountain and feel like you could reach out and touch it... or walk to it in 10 minutes.

Mom was the most busy unpacking my worldly possessions and stuffing them into the nooks and crannies of my dorm room. She seemed especially bent on showing me where she had put all my OTC meds. Her biggest concern was that when I became ill, I knew where to find everything. Laundry was second... what to do and not do.

Parting ways on Monday felt very strange. There was the obligatory last minute list of instructions about staying safe, eating well and studying hard. The long hugs came after there were no more words to say. Watching the maroon car pull away, down College Hill and eventually out of sight, resulted in the oddest concoction of emotions I had ever experienced, even to this day.

It was probably then that I realized that my steps no longer had direct guidance from Mom and Dad. It was the first quantum step toward independence. All the adrenalin was mixed with a "soft" kind of sadness over the notion that I was no longer a permanent resident of 78 Sutton. I suddenly felt intensely lonely... and at the same time, thrilled and feeling like the greatest adventure of my life lay ahead.....

My dorm room faced the inner courtyard in the fall semester, but by the spring, I moved to the top floor in a suite called Poland 602. My dorm room window had a spectacular view of Burke Mountain and the village of Lyndonville in the valley below us. The view was so stunning that focusing on academics there was next to impossible, so I spent most of my study time in the library. However it was that same view that made me sign up for the same room year after year. Poland 602 also had the advantage of being one of the highest points on campus. That was just high enough to pull in an FM radio signal from a Boston pop station that was also popular with a few other suite mates from the Boston area. The reception was reasonably clear in only the top half of one window in the suite's common living room. Pull the radio down from that one sweet spot and the sounds of Boston's WVBF-FM (now known as WROR) faded away.

While broadcast meteorology was my career goal, I still had a love for radio and immediately immersed myself as a member of the student-run, on-campus radio station, WWLR-FM. In addition to a weekly on-air DJ shift, I covered a few of the weekday evening newscasts. In my sophomore year, I started a top-twenty countdown called the NEK-20 (NEK stands for "Northeast Kingdom," a term commonly used to describe the northeast corner of Vermont). It was through that radio program that a Divinely appointed intersection of two people would result in a life-long friendship.

Saturday, November 11, 1978. It was a typical early November weekend on campus. Saturday was my day to goof off. Unless there was one of Dr. Muzzey's grueling calculus problem sets to finish, I let my books collect at least a day's worth of dust. After a late breakfast, I began preparing for the NEK-20.

During the program a young gentlemen, roughly my age as best as I could tell, wandered into the radio station's office. I could see him through the soundproof window just beyond the control board. He seemed to be looking around for someone. Since I was the only one there at the time, I waved him into the studio. It was quickly apparent to me that he was not only comfortable in the studio, but thrived in the environment. This guy was what we in the business call a "radiophile."

Bob Gilmore

Bob walked into the studio and introduced himself. He had driven up to Lyndonville from southern Connecticut with his cousin who was perusing the campus to see what he could find since

Lyndon State was on his short list. Before Bob found the broadcast studio on campus, he was scanning the dial to see what kind of local radio programs he could find. To his delight he found my locally produced pop music countdown, the NEK-20. He and his cousin finally found the building from which the station was broadcasting. Before coming into the Vail Center, he popped a blank audio cassette into his portable radio recorder to capture the episode of the NEK-20 that precipitated an instant friendship.

Being a radiophile myself, Bob and I found instant common ground. We traded stories about "DX'ing," that is, trying to pull in and identify distant AM radio signals from all over the United States. I had been having fun doing this for years while I was in high school. Working with a very sensitive radio and an antenna that was literally wound around the roof of our house, I delighted in listening to radio stations from as far away as Chicago, Fort Wayne, Nashville and occasionally Denver. Until that day, I had never met anyone who had the same level of excitement for DX'ing. It was almost as if I were looking at myself in the mirror in that regard.

Bob stayed for quite some time before his cousin strolled in. Lyndonville was only one of several stops in northern New England for them and they had to head to their next stop in Maine. Bob and I exchanged addresses and we vowed to stay in touch. Having to man the studio to finish the second hour of the program, they parted with a wave through the soundproof window and disappeared.

In the months that followed, Bob and I corresponded once or twice by mail. The class load was heavy, so scribbling a quick note home every few days became difficult, and writing to friends became a luxury that I didn't have the time to enjoy often. Add the element of romance with a girl who, in the years ahead, would become my wife and you suddenly have life traveling at the speed of light. In the blur of my sophomore year, I somehow lost Bob's address. I never wrote it down in my address book. It was written on a scrap of paper or a book cover that ultimately found the trash can before I realized that I was tossing something that could never be replaced.

Two years had passed. In June of 1980, a new weather forecasting firm was looking for a few college meteorology students to help feed weekend weather to a dozen radio stations in New England by phone. It was a great opportunity to get back on the radio during the summer months and to make a little extra book money for my upcoming senior year.

The feeds began every Saturday and Sunday morning at 4:55 AM and each station had a specific call time. One of the stations was WWCO-AM in Bridgeport, Connecticut. After each feed, we used a specific tag line and our names. WWCO was the last station on the list of twelve.

"For WWCO and the New England Weather Network, I'm meteorologist André Bernier."

That was the tag line for the last station on the list before heading up to the kitchen to have breakfast with my parents and brother. It was satisfying to be back on the radio doing forecasts, but for the first time, I was getting paid to do it. I was pleased that the first weekend went so seamlessly and without any issues.

I was scheduled to do the following weekend feed as well. Since the weekend prior had gone so well, it felt like I was slipping right into a well-etched groove. That second Sunday morning feed would prove to be very different. After finishing up with my tag line for WWCO, the DJ picked up the phone and before I had a chance to say goodbye, he asked me a question that will forever ring in my ears.

"Are you the André Bernier that goes to Lyndon State College in Vermont?"

The question stunned me. How does a DJ in Bridgeport, Connecticut know that I attend LSC? I told him that I was, but before I could get another befuddled word out of my mouth, the DJ then told me that he was Bob Gilmore, the gentleman who visited the college campus studios almost two years earlier. He mentioned that something sounded very familiar last week when he took the weather feed, but was not able to make the connection until after he hung up the phone. Bob was determined to ask me the following Sunday morning. We were both elated that, by Divine appointment, our paths had crossed once again. Bob and I exchanged addresses and phone numbers and vowed to never lose touch.

In hindsight, so many things had to have been in place for this re-introduction. Bob had to be working the overnight shift on Sunday morning at a specific radio station. A college classmate had to have recommended me to Tom Chisolm, the meteorologist who started the new radio weather company, to help on weekends. I had to have weekends available. Computing the chance of these three variables alone placed our re-introduction at more than million to one.

The start of my senior year in Vermont was miserable enough without the company of my wife-to-be while she spent a semester at Purdue University. Add moving into a single dorm room in a suite whose occupants' only interest was to test the pain threshold of their ears while listening to the Ramones into the wee hours of every morning and it was the most forgettable semester of my college experience. The only redemption of that semester was getting reacquainted with Bob. He took the three-and-a-half hour trek north on several occasions and even picked up one of the radio shifts at WWLR one Sunday afternoon before heading back to Connecticut. Having radio in common was just the tip of the iceberg. Our friendship continued to grow into one of those rare friendships that go well beyond the normal. It was as if our entire family adopted him and he adopted us.

I find it humorous and ironic that as I write this story, it is exactly thirty years to the day that Bob Gilmore first walked into the campus radio station to find the face behind the voice of the NEK-20. Who would have ever thought at the time that, thirty years later, I would listen to that very NEK-20 broadcast on something called an iPod in my car? On the flip side, I just learned that Bob watched our ten o'clock television newscast from his computer at his Connecticut home. Neither of us ever imagined the kinds of changes in technology that we would witness. All that aside, both of us still scan the AM radio dial at night. Once a radiophile, always a radiophile.

Bob Brickey

If someone asked you what the most thoughtful gift you have ever received, chances are you would be able to answer quickly. You might even think of several that were particularly meaningful. It's an interesting question since most of the time the gift was not exceptionally expensive.

For me, three gifts stand out as strikingly thoughtful. The first was when I was about ten years old. It was my birthday on a beautiful spring evening. My father was not yet home from work and my mother had made a wonderful dinner complete with a birthday cake of my choice as was her custom. Dad was working late, and so the rest of us enjoyed dinner and cake followed by a few birthday gifts. I do not remember any of them except for one which did not arrive until Dad arrived home just as the dishes were being cleared. In his hands was a brown paper bag. With a smile, he gave it to me and wished me a happy birthday. Inside the bag was the Tru-Temp outdoor thermometer I had been eyeing at a local store. He then told me that he would spend Saturday morning installing it wherever I wanted it. True to his word, he patiently let me try out a number of different locations as he stepped up a ladder on the outside of the house. That thermometer could not have cost much more than a few dollars, but it was the most thoughtful gift since he took the time to place it wherever I wanted, knowing full well that I would incessantly check the temperature on it for years to come.

The second gift came from a Lyndon State classmate whom I met in my sophomore year. His name is Bob Brickey.

Poland 602 was a unique college suite. We all valued those things for which we were there, namely an education, but with a delightful balance. Unlike many suites, ours was usually pretty quiet after eleven o'clock. The wildest that our Fridays and Saturdays became was an under control party that went to midnight. Aside from those who called Poland 602 "home," others would find it a pleasant place to socialize.

Bob was one of our suitemates with his roommate, Steve. In leisure time, Bob and Steve were rarely apart and were a loveable, modern day version of Starsky and Hutch, best friends whose countenance was forever joyful. I cannot remember a single instance where either of them sported anything less than a genuine smile.

December is always an active month in a college setting, but in my case it was non-stop in my sophomore year. In addition to studying for finals, it was the month that Glen Salegna and I had planned and arranged a giant student disco party in the college's student center. Glen had purchased the equipment during the summer. Being more than fond of urban contemporary music, I was more than eager to help make all the arrangements through the college. All this was happening when I discovered that one of my college radio colleagues was roommate with the girl that had captured my attention. She agreed to try to convince her to come to the disco party, a task that she not only accomplished, but that led to the start of a journey with a beautiful, blue-eyed beauty who would one day become my wife and life partner.

Without any calculus courses to weigh me down that semester, I was not tempted to pull any "all nighters" to study for finals. The majority of my exams were scheduled at the end of the week before Christmas break. With every passing day, the campus became quieter and quieter. By Thursday, it was downright spooky. Fortunately, Poland 602 still had a fair number of students waiting to take exams. It was almost as if all of us had the whole campus to ourselves.

Later that evening, the unusual silence of Poland 602 was broken by the sounds of two jovial souls who were singing Christmas songs and carrying several bags of goods. It was Bob and Steve. If it had been any other time of year, we might have suspected that they had sampled a little too much of the Baldwin sisters' secret recipe eggnog. That wasn't the case at all. Both had rivers of Christmas joy bubbling out of them, but there was something else going on too. Their fortissimo singing seemed to call everyone out of their rooms. It looked as if they had something up their sleeves and couldn't wait to reveal it. We were all about to find out.

With only a very short introduction, we were all informed that they had been on a Christmas shopping spree and returned with a special gift for each one of us. With each gift came broad smiles. Then it was my turn. Bob pulled out a box and handed it to me. As I unwrapped the gift, I saw a box of amaretto liqueur. I was amazed. Each gift given had an extraordinary level of thought behind it. They had grown to know me well enough to observe that amaretto was one of my favorite liqueurs and still is. It warmed my heart to the very core to know that Bob and Steve blew all the money that they had to get us each a gift that had a great deal of thought behind it. They were broke, but as happy as clams at high tide. Watching their joy was a meaningful lesson in how to give gifts to others. That lesson still ministers to me today.

Only one other gift that rose to that level came, once again, from my father. It was while we were on a family weekend trip to Burke Mountain, Vermont, more than ten years after graduating from Lyndon State. The gift was a box of Alka-Seltzer from The Willey's Store in Greensboro, Vermont. After a debilitating migraine began to slowly subside, we all took the dirt road short cut over Stannard Mountain to Greensboro to see our friends, the Hurst family, who owned the fully-stocked country store. Dad was on a mission. He looked up and down all the aisles looking for something while the rest of us occupied our time by saying hello to the family members that were there and looking for a souvenir or two to bring back home. When we all reconvened where the car was parked, Dad once again gave me an unassuming brown paper bag with a box of Alka Seltzer. Being a man of modest means, I knew that he had spent more than half of what was in his wallet in order to bring me relief.

Dad went home to be with the Lord in December of 2003 at the age of eighty-eight. To this day, the unopened box of Alka-Seltzer sits in a special place as a reminder of a father's love for his son.

Bob Brickey and I still exchange calls, letters and Christmas cards. A decade after graduating, I even had the opportunity to have breakfast with him when I was driving from Ohio to meet my family for another weekend getaway at Burke Mountain. He was still full of the joy of life, and his family equally delightful. There is an old adage that says that one cannot enter a smoke-filled room without emerging with the smell of smoke on his clothes. Without even knowing it, Bob's joy and generosity spilled onto others, including me.

The Old Man In The Car

Without intentional care to protect joy as an attribute independent of one's circumstances, joy can vanish in a heartbeat. Such was the case not even a week after Bob Brickey's thoughtful gift waited for me back in Poland 602.

There are likely millions and millions of people with whom we all have had extremely brief encounters of several seconds. Most of them happen unconsciously as we walk about our daily activities. You can rack up thousands of them if you walk to the park for lunch on a warm spring day in the city.

Every once in a very rare while, one of these brief encounters will change your heart.

It was Christmas time in New Bedford and I was home on college break. For a reason that now escapes me and is unimportant anyway, I was driving from near St. Anthony's Church on Acushnet Avenue back to my parent's house. Being a meteorology major, it's no surprise that I remember the skies as being gloomy gray and damp. It was cool but not cold. Unlike the heavy snow pack on the college campus, there was no snow on the ground anywhere. It was going to be a snowless Christmas.

I was zigzagging through familiar streets like Nye and Bullard, eventually into the narrow streets passing by the now-abandoned textile mills where very little traffic is seen. As I was preparing to make a right turn through one of the intersections, another vehicle came barreling through the stop sign making a left turn. The turn was so broad that I realized, without quick action, his car would hit mine.

The brakes on the 1972 Caliente we had were always one of the best features of the car. Without thinking, the car went from moving to a dead stop with the obligatory screeching tires. He stopped in the middle of the intersection, and now we were looking at each other, eyeball to eyeball through our side windows. I was fit to be tied and could feel my blood pressure rising in a near rage of anger. I was going to tell this guy off.

I rolled down my window. Then he rolled down his window, slowly, as an older man would. As his window hit the top of the door's frame, I took a deep breath in and was ready to launch an assault of the tongue.

Just before my first word came out, the old man looked at me, smiled tenderly, raised his left hand in a gesture of good will and slowly said, "Merry Christmas."

I was so stunned that the breath I had stored up for the assault was frozen in my lungs.

The man's soft blue eyes and weathered face was asking for forgiveness in the most creative way I had ever witnessed. In the Bible, Solomon wrote that "a soft answer turneth away wrath: but grievous words stir up anger," (Proverbs 15:1, KJV). This old man became that Scripture passage.

The breath I took in seemed to disappear without any exhale. In the few seconds it took me to respond, the spirit of peace warmed me from inside out. I, too, started to smile and was able to finally respond.

"Merry Christmas."

We both rolled up our windows and moved on. As I pulled away from him, I couldn't help myself from laughing out loud. The dichotomy of emotions was so extreme that it was funny. Most importantly, he was an effective administrator of God's Word who spoke life and beauty into a situation that needed it.

An old man. A gentle answer. A changed heart. I wish I knew his name. I'm sure someday I will.

Kurt Singer

Ever since I can remember, I enjoyed writing. One of the earliest adventures in writing was my elaborate digital watch idea that I described in chapter one. Not long after, my sister's manual typewriter fascinated me and I would spend hours at a time banging out weather forecasts and logs in slow, hunt-and-peck fashion.

Aside from logging weather statistics beginning in the 1960s, I would also jot side notes on days where something significant happened. One might call it journaling light. Call it what you will, but those notes allow me to remember each of those days as if they happened only a few moments ago. Up to this point, most of my writing had a practical application. Yet there was a dimension of it that seemed dormant until my college days.

Long before the days of the Internet, the exercise of running from line to line and signing up for core and elective courses was a necessary albeit boring task. Once I secured my core classes, perusing the electives became a bit more stimulating. There was a course offering called, "Creative Writing," taught by Prof. Kurt Singer. After reading the description, something came to life in me. While it was late in the sign-up process, I was pleased to find a few spots still open.

I looked forward to my classes in calculus, climatology, physics and chemistry. They turned out to be the stretching mental challenge that I envisioned. But something very different happened walking into the classroom for "Creative Writing." While this class was going to motivate and challenge us in how we wrote, Prof. Singer let his own passion for good writing set a delightful undercurrent in motion that none of us in that room could resist. Our minds were carried away into other worlds as each class began with his reading a short story, a poem or part of a great literary work, followed by a discussion about that work and how it resonated with us. There were a number of times where he would read some of his own work. He read with such passion, drilling deep into the heart of each work that, in between each sentence and breath, you could hear a pin drop. Each of us yearned to use words to paint the kind of imagery that was so clear and crisp that we could touch it.

Our assignments were wide and varied and always challenged each of us to be more effective masters of language. Some professors would have approached creative writing as a dry, technical skill. Prof. Singer would have none of that. While there was an appropriate place for technical skill, he went to lengths to teach us that exceptional writing is an art form. Developing the artist in us was something in which he took joy.

There were days when, as we settled into class and awaited

Prof. Singer's arrival, we would buzz about the assignment he gave us. His love for the art of writing was so infectious that every student had something ready to share. One would figure that a broadcast meteorology student who was already comfortable with live radio would be comfortable with reading his own work with twenty other students and a professor, but that was not the case at all. When Prof. Singer asked me if I would share what I had written, the first sentence or two were read boldly as if I were on the radio. Having 22 pairs of eyes that were focused directly on me changed that. Becoming self-aware to a fault produced far more adrenalin than I wanted and within minutes I was gasping for breath in between sentences. I went from expressing my thoughts clearly to babbling mindless words and praying that Prof. Singer would tell me that it was all right to stop. He did, and it always felt like a wonderful rescue.

Toward the end of the semester I was able to extend the time before the mindless drivel began to creep in, but none of that mattered in Prof. Singer's class. He was truly much more interested in how we used words to paint mind images or to capture an emotion or feeling. Constructive critique always came with encouragement to enjoy the journey of using words. There wasn't a single classmate I ever met who did not like his creative writing class even if they took it to satisfy elective requirements.

Prof. Singer had another perk available to his students. Anyone who was able to get an article published in any periodical received extra credit. During one of our mid-semester breaks, an article that I had submitted to the *National Weather Digest* about a severe thunderstorm outbreak in southern New England had received the thumbs-up. The article was one of the features in the quarterly periodical for general weather enthusiasts. It was more of a technical article that I was certain was not the kind that Prof. Singer had in mind. Nonetheless, I gave him a copy of the article only to share the excitement of being published. I never expected him to consider it for his publishing perk, but much to my surprise, not only did he give me extra credit, but he shared the news with my classmates. He told me that style and subject was never a consideration. It was using words well enough to paint the kind of image that would net an approval from an editor.

After graduation, while beginning my career as a broadcast meteorologist in Iowa, I had little time to write. Yet a seed had been planted in that third-floor classroom that was waiting for the right catalyst to make it germinate. The soil around that seed began to warm during one of my vacations to New England. My parents were both particularly bent on telling me and my siblings some of the stories from their youth. While we had all heard the stories time and again, we never grew tired of them. Many of them were so comical that, in our hysteria, we were weak-kneed with tears streaming down from our faces.

On the early morning of our departure back to Ohio, my parents were up and fixing us a hearty breakfast before our twelve-hour journey began. As I drank my coffee and as my nose caressed the aroma of the bacon on the skillet, they began telling a few more anecdotes from years long gone. As they spun their tales, an odd sense of melancholy sat in the pit of my stomach. I couldn't help thinking that someday all these wonderful stories would fade into oblivion as our memories faded and the people in our lives crossed over that inevitable eternal curtain.

With dawn beginning to splash color on the eastern horizon and with our bellies full, we began our drive west. The quiet drone of the engine was the only sound in the car as my wife closed her eyes to slumber. Less than an hour later, as the sun came closer to announcing a new day by rising above the horizon, the colors in my rearview mirror were simply stunning. The iridescent oranges, pinks and reds made me marvel at God's creative artwork. It was a moment of worship, and it was the catalyst that made the swelling seed planted in my soul push through the soil to capture the first brilliant rays of the sun as it broke the horizon. The stories we were entertained with all week didn't have to die on the vine. I had them fresh in my mind and I could preserve them for future generations. I had the power. The power was in the written word. A book was conceived. The melancholy was gone, replaced by the kind of excitement a child gets heading into a candy store. That very night, I fired up my Apple Macintosh II and immediately started the first few pages of what would end up being a private, self-published book that was a Christmas gift to my family two years later.

The title, "A Bucket Of Blue Steam," came from a wildly funny restaurant story that my father told us on New Year's Eve night in 1983 while I was home on vacation from "The Weather Channel" in Atlanta. It was a story that my brother and I nearly missed since we had been invited to a New Year's Eve party hosted by long-time school classmates only a block and a half away, something we were both looking forward to. Not long before we planned to head out that Saturday night, we made ourselves comfortable in our parent's living room. Without warning, Mom and Dad caught a tidal wave of anecdotal storytelling. One after another, they amazed us since much of it was brand-new material the likes of which we had never heard in our lives. It was sheer joy to see them so animated while we learned even more about them.

Minutes turned to hours. Before we realized it, 1984 was about to be ushered in, and suddenly showing up to a New Year's Eve party after midnight seemed to violate protocol - strange at the very least and rude at the very most. Instead, we retired to bed armed with more new material for a book that was still about a decade away from being published.

When the book finally neared completion, I had to share the news with the professor since he planted the seed. Prof. Singer was the first person outside my family to whom I sent a copy. He not only read the book with great delight, but he sent me a delightful letter highlighting his favorite chapters. It began a very long exchange of letters and cards. I was delighted to receive and read a number of books that he published during that time. Prof. Singer went from being my English professor, to mentor, and to peer and friend. The seed that he planted was now a small tree with roots.

Beyond the tales of our family, there was something else simmering under the surface. I desired to take people to a place that only existed in a deep nook in my soul. As much as I enjoyed great poetry, it was definitely not my gift. So how do I express it? How do I tap into that place in such a way the reader is engaged?

The outlet became apparent in 1997. After several meetings with radio station general manager, Dick Lee, from WCRF in Cleveland, and with about a year's worth of research, Dick agreed to entertain the possibility of creating a new radio program. Modeled after a successful program out of Minneapolis called, "Saturday Night," and similar to Garrison Keillor's, "A Prairie Home Companion," our program called "Soup Du Jour" would be music, dramatic and comedic skits and stories - performed as a radio broadcast before a live theater audience. It was from the radio broadcast that a storyline was born about the people of the cozy, rural town of Pilaf, Ohio.

While the storyline was fiction, its root was that secluded nook in my soul that, until that time, found no means of expression. The taproot of the tree burrowed into that place and began to draw what it needed to grow. God had placed this inspirational deposit in an inner alcove, slowly accumulating dividends. By the time Pilaf was born, there was a wealth of treasure waiting. No one recognized this better than Prof. Singer who affirmed this in so many ways over the years.

I have two special correspondences from him that, to this day, have a special place in my office. The first came in a large padded envelope. I could feel that it was a book. I anticipated that it was a new book of his poems and smiled. What I found was something that made me laugh out loud. It was a recipe book that he had found at a local garage sale entitled, *Pilaf, Risotto and Other Ways With Rice*. His inscription on the inside cover was priceless:

"To André – inhabitant of Pilaf, U.S.A."

The second came in the form of a photograph slipped into a note card. In the photo is a grand looking maple tree, tall and stately, very close to Bailey's & Burke, a popular Vermont country store in the sleepy hollow of East Burke, Vermont. It was the model for a majestic tree that took center stage in "Chapter Five" of my book, *Welcome To Pilaf*, the chapter from which the title came. I was amazed, but not surprised that Prof. Singer knew.

I was hoping he would read this book someday. That was not to be. As I was wrapping up this chapter, I received word from his lovely bride that he had taken flight into eternity. While he never had the chance to see so much as one word of this book, I am convinced that he received something far greater from our eternal Father, whom he embraced. Just as Moses was shown the Promised Land by God Himself from the top of a mountain, I have a hunch that Kurt Singer was shown a field ripe with a harvest as far as the eye can see. A harvest that came from decades of planting his uncountable seeds of passion, encouragement and joy not to mention the seeds of love for his craft and his students.

Surely a journey well done, good and faithful servant.

The Beauty Of One Red Rose

Much like living on the windward side of Lake Erie in December, January and February, Vermont is strikingly monochromatic in the winter. While the snow banks steadily grow, snowfalls usually occur only a couple of inches at a time. Because temperatures rarely climb above freezing, the snowscape rules until the mud season arrives when the snow finally melts.

The mountainous terrain also helped to keep the skies cloud-shrouded most of the time. I still remember the quiet depression and irritation of a thirty-day stretch when not a single ray of sunshine had graced our campus. At the end of that thirtieth day and while sitting down for dinner in the Stevens Dining Hall, one small, punched-out hole in the overcast allowed a small beam of sunlight to illuminate a small spot in the village below us. The usual cacophony of the dining hall was quelled. It was beautiful. Much to everyone's surprise the hole maneuvered so that, for less than a minute, a burst of bright sunshine filled the dining hall with its blinding light. Within seconds, everyone stopped eating, rose from their seats and gave the sunny cameo a standing ovation. Suddenly the world was all right again.

That's what made Valentine's Day, 1979 most unusual. While the bitter winds insisted on whipping up swirls of snow into the air, the sky was as azure blue as it could be. The sunlight was so convincing that if it were not for my rosy cheeks, runny nose and arctic parka, I might have thought that I was in the Caribbean.

For over a year, another meteorology student, one year my junior, had captured my heart. Even before Sally and I had the opportunity to meet, I sensed something special about her. My excitement grew when I discovered that her roommate was Suzie Roach, a friend of mine who had a radio shift at the college radio station. I asked her if she would be willing to be an underground matchmaker and she agreed to try.

Glen Salegna was a classmate who owned a portable DJ system and I enjoyed the art of club mixing. Glen brought his system to the college and we convinced the college to let us hold a disco dance party in the student center on a Friday night. On that night, I was counting on my friend to convince Sally to come for a little while. Glen knew that I was going to be watching out for her and that when she arrived, he would take over. That would give me enough time to pull her onto the dance floor so that I could introduce myself. That was "Part One" of my plan. If "Part One" succeeded, then Glen knew to proceed with "Part Two." Sally arrived and I wasted little time. I went over and pulled her up out of her chair and onto the dance floor. Great dance music, a great light show, and a dance partner with the most beautiful blue eyes I had ever seen made that moment almost perfect. Perfect would depend on "Part Two."

After a few minutes, I glanced over to the stage where Glen was sporting a smile as he glanced back. "Part Two" was ready. The dance song faded and the next one started. As prescribed, Glen slowed it down with a perfectly timed, slow, romantic song. Sally began to move toward the sideline, but I insisted on staying on the floor. She did, and then the night was perfect.

A week later, we had our first bona fide date at The Old Cutter Inn near Burke Mountain. My sense was right. Sally was special in every way.

Now it was St. Valentine's Day and I wanted to surprise her with something, but to a student on a very tight budget, that something was no more than one or two red roses. With no car and no one that I knew that was driving into the "Ville," my only option was to make the two-mile descent on foot. The thought of it aroused a sense of adventure and chivalry, and the arctic whistles became a mere inconvenience.

In downtown Lyndonville, I bought one red rose at the local florist shop on Depot Street. In her kindness, the clerk took extra care and measures to garnish and frame the rose. It looked simple but elegant. Thanking her, I started the ascent back up to the campus. The wind and arctic chill seemed to have bigger teeth compared to my walk down. Concerned that the rose would be damaged by the frozen air, I tucked it inside my parka. I wasn't sure what would be worse, a rose limp from exposure to the crisp air or a flattened rose from being inside my parka.

The road up to the college was deserted so the only sounds I heard during my ascent to the campus were of the wind and my breath. It gave me time to second-guess such a modest gift even though it was the best I could do at the time.

My body was growing numb from the cold when I heard the sound of an approaching vehicle. No sooner did it pass me than it came to a stop. A older woman, probably around sixty, rolled down her window.

"You look pretty cold. Can I drive you up to the college?"

"That would be great. I truly appreciate it."

Once inside her delightfully warm car, she started up the hill as I carefully took the rose out from under my parka to see if there was any wear from being pressed.

"That must be for someone special."

"Oh, it is."

I didn't know what else to say. At that point, I was just happy to escape from the brutal cold. There was silence for a minute, then the woman turned to me with a comforting smile and said something I will forever remember.

"That sure is a lovely rose. You know a single, beautiful rose like that is so much better than a dozen. There is great beauty in simplicity. I am absolutely certain that your special someone is going to love it and what you went through to get it."

It was as if she knew exactly what I was feeling and thinking while walking up that icy road.

"Do you really think so?"

"I know it."

I can't remember if she ever introduced herself. Even if she did, my brain was so cold that it would have never retained it. With a smile and a wave she dropped me off at the college and continued on her way.

Lyndonville is a very small college town. Everyone seemed to know everyone else. You could easily run into almost everyone who lived there at the town grocery store, White Market, at one time or another, yet I had never seen my kind chauffeur before nor had I ever seen her car. I was a sophomore. For two and a half years following that St. Valentine's Day, I kept an eye out for her on the road where she had offered refuge from the icy winds. I had hoped to give her another friendly wave of thanks and to let her know that she was right, but I never saw her again.

Hebrews 13:2 tells us that sometimes we entertain angels without knowing it. There are a number of encounters I have experienced over the decades that, even today, I still wonder about. It doesn't matter. Whether this encounter was angelic or earthly, it was a Divine appointment like those I have come to learn about with every person who crosses my path or every phone call I receive at work. Every day is filled with them, and it has truly changed the way I journey through every day given to me as a gift.

Chapter 4

Watching The Corn Grow

In May of 1981, I was busy with the task of preparing for final exams, graduation, and a transition from college life to a professional one.

Very early in the year I was, like all the students, busy with the additional task of writing cover letters, updating resumés and sending out videotapes to television stations that had openings for a weather anchor. I was concentrating my efforts on the northeastern part of the United States, but not totally abandoning all the options. I was willing to begin in a very small market just to stay in the northeast. Given that the chances of landing your first job get better as the market gets smaller, I remember sending a resumé and tape to a small television station in Johnstown, Pennsylvania in addition to other larger markets that also had openings. My prayers were long and hard for Johnstown and I thought I had a decent chance of at least an interview.

The day came when there was a letter in my post office box from Johnstown. Could it be a letter asking me to call them at my earliest convenience? It proved otherwise. It contained a cordial but very standard form letter informing me that I was not quite what they were looking for. I had received other letters like it in previous weeks but this one was difficult to process.

If market size "One Hundred" wasn't interested in my work, who would be?

As easy as it would have been to quit, my passion for weathercasting told me to press on. Videotapes and resumés continued to fly out of my hands and into those of the postal clerk at the Lyndonville post office. It got to the point where I could no longer remember which videotape I sent to which job opening, something over which I liked having more control. As it turned out, that's what likely helped me land my first job offer.

In mid-March of that year, I received a phone call on the dorm's shared phone from Bob Jackson. He introduced himself as the news director for WMT-TV-2 in Cedar Rapids, Iowa. After an exchange of pleasantries, he asked if I would consider coming out to Iowa for a face-to-face interview. Without reservation, I jumped at the opportunity.... but, Iowa? It was much farther than I had hoped to travel for my first job.

On Sunday, March 29, 1981, it was Sally who drove me to Burlington, Vermont's airport, to catch a flight to Cedar Rapids via Chicago. The flight to Chicago was uneventful but the second leg was much more than what I bargained for. The flight from Chicago to Cedar Rapids was on a small prop puddle jumper operated by now defunct Mississippi Valley Airlines. My seat assignment was near the rear of the aircraft. Not having flown much up to that point, it was somewhat disconcerting to see the top portion of the fuselage jerk from left to right in the turbulence while taking off from Chicago. It was loud and it was bumpy. Yet I marveled as I saw the beautiful Illinois and Iowa farmland for the first time in my life. There was just something about its intrinsic serenity that beckoned a convincing invitation to begin the first leg of my professional career.

Bob Jackson was there to meet me. The airport, which reminded me of my hometown airport in New Bedford, was as quiet as one would expect in Iowa on a Sunday. The corn was just beginning to germinate in some fields and the smell of organic earth permeated everything as I waited for Bob to pull the car around.

Cedar Rapids was a beautiful little town. As we drove into the downtown, the scents of bread baking in the oven were most unusual. Where was this coming from? Bob explained that when winds were west or northwest, the scents from the city's Quaker Oats plant caressed the city with smells that were reminiscent of those you'd expect entering your favorite bakery. He did warn me, however, of a less appealing odor that a humid, south or southwest wind would bring in from the nearby slaughter house in that direction, a smell I would not sample until my move there later that summer.

I was still wondering why a major powerhouse television station, Number One in the ratings for decades and in a market size much larger than those from which most of my rejection letters came would have been so interested in interviewing me. As the interview that quiet Sunday afternoon progressed, I saw the videotape I had sent on his desk. We watched it together and suddenly it all made sense.

The weathercast from the college's television newscast that day had a particularly lengthy focus on agricultural impacts of the weather in the Midwest and Northeast. It was, in my opinion, not my best work. In the mad rush to send tapes and resumés out to job openings, I grabbed whatever was available. In hindsight it was yet more evidence of the Divine Hand of God guiding my steps to where He wanted me to go.

After a comfortable stay at Stouffer's Four Seasons Hotel, we continued with the interview on Monday, meeting Kelly Atherton, the station's general manager and doing a screen test using one of the station's news anchors on their set. As nervous as I was, I was convincing enough to be offered a three-year contract. I was thrilled. Suddenly, there was chaos and pandemonium in the newsroom. At 1:30 Central Time, we both left Bob's office to watch the replays of President Ronald Reagan being shot outside the Washington Hilton Hotel where he had just given a speech at an AFL-CIO luncheon. My interview was over. There was news to report and the news hive was buzzing with activity.

Sally picked me up at Burlington airport that evening. It was evident that unless Burlington, Manchester, or any smaller northeast market called in the next few days, I would be heading to the Hawkeye State right after graduation in a few months.

One of the conditions on which the job was offered was that I shave my mustache. WMT-TV did not allow facial hair. I did not like that prospect as it took me a very long time to grow it during my college years, but they signed the paychecks and insisted on clean-shaven talent. Much sooner than I needed to, I shaved off my mustache to try to get used to it. The added time never bought me anything. My facial hair would be gone only as long as it had to be. I simply never got used to it.

As May approached, a graduating classmate told me that I would not be going out to Cedar Rapids alone. Brian Durst, also a senior meteorology major, had just been offered a job at KCRG-TV, the competition. I was thrilled that I would have some company in a city that was a thousand miles farther from home than I had ever been, even though he would end up going head-to-head with me in the same weekend time slot.

The brief window between graduation and the trip to Iowa was but a breathy mist. In the few short days I was back home in New Bedford my mother and father tried to help me pack what I would need to get started on my own. While I no longer remember the moving truck and those belongings that were shipped west, I do remember the new suit that they bought for me and that my mother tailored while I stood on the kitchen table.

It would soon be my birthday, May 22nd, and much to my family's disappointment, I could not stay long enough to celebrate it at home. Cedar Rapids was asking that I arrive as quickly as I could after graduation. The lilacs were in bloom filling the air with that wonderful spring aroma and I wondered if Iowa had any lilac bushes. I didn't know. The only photos of Iowa I ever saw had corn and lots of it, and I did not get to see much of Cedar Rapids during my fly-in, fly-out interview. It was one of many nervous thoughts that crowded my thinking as I finished packing.

Deciding I would wait to buy a car until after arriving in Iowa, Sally kept me company and drove what I could fit in her car, stopping for one day in Cleveland at her parent's home before finishing the trek to corn country.

The apartment I would eventually be renting on Blake Road S.E. was being prepared. One of my classmates in the meteorology program at Lyndon State had a brother whose close friend not only lived in Cedar Rapids, but was an employee of WMT-TV and was planning to rent the upper floor of his home. It didn't take too long to contact Demetrius Hodges and to express an interest in the arrangement. Before graduating, the ducks lined up. I had a job in my field and I had an apartment to rent. The only thing remaining for Demetrius to install in the upstairs was a shower which he put on the fast track knowing a renter would be coming soon.

The assumption that WMT would put me up at the Four Seasons Hotel for two or three weeks while I waited to move into my apartment was a bad one. While I can't remember the name of the motel, it was certainly not of the same caliber as the place to which they treated me during my interview. While very workable, it was extremely basic. To this day, I still remember the smell of the motel hallway. My memory is jarred whenever I encounter it at other hotels and motels, and I get transported back to Cedar Rapids and what was going through my mind at the time. The butterflies flutter all over again.

On the other hand, the smell of the brand new 1981 Ford Mustang I bought was a good one. It was a standard without an air conditioner and with manual windows. But that did not bother me at all. It was my first credit purchase ever. The price tag was $2,800 new. At the time, I thought that was a moderately steep figure, but never again would I see new cars sold for that kind of price tag. It was the first real symbol of independence for me and so that Mustang was always washed and waxed once or twice a month. It was through that car that I also had a taste of the real world when my very sporty hubcaps were stolen one day when I parked it on the side of the apartment complex that I lived in later that summer. From that day on, my car was always parked in front where I could see it from my living room window.

WMT wasted no time in getting me settled and on-air. My first weekend evening weathercast is something I'd rather bury deep in my memory garden. It wasn't a bad weathercast, mind you, but there was one faux pas by which I will forever remember it. Admittedly nervous, I kept pointing to the state weather map (then a painted map of Iowa on which you drew with markers) and kept calling "Iowa," "Ohio." My only connection to Ohio was having a girlfriend who grew up in Ohio and who still went home there in the summers. Good grief. What would the audience think of the new weather babbler who did not even know what state he was in?

Dave Towne

I first met Dave during the second day of my interview with Bob Jackson, the day President Reagan was shot. The weather was warm and sultry on this late March day and the radar showed tall thunderstorms in western Iowa. Wanting to make a good impression on the meteorologist I'd be working with, I remember engaging him in conversation about that afternoon's thunderstorm risk. Dave was pleasant and did not offer resistance to my concern over the storms even though they did not pose a threat. Instead, he treated me with respect as we talked "weather," peer-to-peer. It was clear that Dave was not threatened by the new kid on the block at all and was perfectly at ease with himself, the kind of confidence I hoped to someday develop. I knew I was going to enjoy working with him. Our friendship began quickly with only this brief visit.

Since Brian had not yet moved to Iowa when I did, it was easy to quickly feel like I was a baby goldfish in a large ocean with shark shadows passing by. I knew no one except Dave and a handful of other people at WMT. Stopping by in the afternoons to spend some time shooting the breeze with Dave and watching him operate was the best thing I could do to temporarily ease my homesickness.

I often tell everyone that my time in Cedar Rapids was the loneliest time of my life. I was far away from my hometown, my friends, my family, and anything familiar. Growing up was no longer an option. It was something I had to do fast. Yet there was something about this complete independence that was refreshing and intoxicating. I loved Cedar Rapids and I hated Cedar Rapids all at the same time. Up until this period in my life's journey, digging deep to explore what makes me tick was something I did not have to do. Life was dictated by everything and everyone around me and I was perfectly comfortable with that, knowing full well that someday that would change. That paradigm shift was suddenly thrust upon me. Having a new friend like Dave made that transition from a college kid to an adult employee and independent member of society easier to navigate.

I could not have been there any longer than a few weeks when my first kick of Midwest thunderstorm reality took a swipe at this native New Englander. It was a quiet Sunday evening. The six o'clock news was done. After dinner, I took a brief walk in a local park and took in the warm, summer breezes and bright sunshine. There wasn't a cloud in the sky anywhere, something I now call NACITS (an acronym that I actually coined in Iowa). The sunset was stunning. Afterwards, I went back to my work and took a quick check of things before drawing the final maps on the board with Rich Art color markers. (Only a few of the maps then were drawn by computer). The National Weather Service radar from Waterloo, Iowa was displayed on a then state-of-the-art color display and delivered by modem (leading edge technology, mind you, in 1981). It showed the customary growing ground clutter pattern as the night skies cooled, or so I thought. As if it were yesterday, I remember delivering that night's weathercast with a bit of whimsy, talking about how beautiful it was and how lovely and quiet the rest of the night would proceed. I returned to the weather office from the studio and the phone was ringing. It was Dave.

"André, have you looked out the window recently?"

"No," I replied, wondering why he asked such a strange question.

"You better go take a look behind the station."

That's all he said, very calmly. Being curious, I did as he suggested. Much to my horror, I saw continuous lightning from a cluster of thunderheads about twenty miles away. How could that be? It was perfectly clear an hour before. I called Dave back and he very gently introduced me to the phenomenon I had studied in college courses before but never personally encountered. The nocturnal (nighttime) thunderstorm, an often severe thunderstorm cluster that develops at night in the Midwest, was no longer classroom theory. I saw its full fury later that night as I drove home wondering if I had just delivered my last weathercast. The newscast was over and redeeming myself would have to wait until Wednesday's noon weathercast. As I reluctantly called Dave back that evening, I received reassurance instead of a reproach. He was even chuckling while giving me the formal introduction to Iowa's famous nocturnal thunderstorms.

Apparently, my arrival in Cedar Rapids was quite a relief to Dave as now he could take some of the vacation time that he was unable to take before due to limited weather staff. As I watched him operate the weekday evening shows with such fluidity in addition to programming one of the first weather graphics computers in the country in the old Basic language, line by line, the mere thought of filling in for his upcoming summer vacations sent me to the bathroom. It felt like a cage full of butterflies on a caffeine overdose had been let loose in my stomach. It was so much to learn. Dave made the process easy and was a great mentor in affirming me along the way.

My face must have been an easy read since he frequently would give me words of encouragement, asking me if everything was all right and telling me in his calming way to "cheer up."

With my apartment on Blake Boulevard ready and the new shower installed in the upstairs bathroom, I was ready to move in. I had the entire upstairs and a separate entrance via the back or the front, with a spot in the two-car, unattached garage behind the house for my Mustang. The spread was so large that the few belongings that I did have did not even come close to making a dent in filling the kitchen, bedroom and dining room. In fact, the living room sat empty the whole time I was there. Add a hardwood floor and the hollowness of my footsteps in that room amplified the homesickness I had to the point that I avoided walking into the room for any reason.

To add sounds of life to the apartment, I ran out to Sears and purchased a television on credit. It was time to build up a credit rating and this was a controlled and safe way to start. When I brought the set home, it either sat on my dinner table or on a set of milk crates that I used as book storage space. I simply did not have the money to buy furniture. I was making $16,000 a year and most of my check went to pay rent, car payments, household expenditures and a monthly payment on a television set. I was lucky to have a few dollars left over for some occasional entertainment or a run to Bishop's Restaurant with Dave and the gang at WMT-TV.

When Dave took his first week-long vacation that summer, I quickly realized how fast we had become friends. The week went by slowly. While I had made some other friends along the way, it wasn't the same. In addition to the pressure of filling in for a well-established, well-liked Iowa television meteorologist, driving back to Blake Road at night when the sun after down was a strange experience. Even more unsettling were the handful of nights that thunderstorms threatened to make my run from the garage to the back door an experience to remember. It wasn't the rain as much as it was the lightning. Never had I seen lightning flash so frequently. It also filled the apartment with thunder that echoed on the wood floors in the big, empty living room. Unlike during the quiet, bright days, the thunder drew my attention to that room as much as I tried to busy myself with other things or to try to fall asleep. Calling my parents in New Bedford crossed my mind on many such nights, but being an hour ahead of Iowa time, I knew calling them would disrupt their sleep. I turned on the television and watched any remotely interesting late-night program until I was tired enough to see if sleep would come.

Demetrius and his wife had no children yet. They were relative newlyweds. But they did have Ivan. I called him, "Ivan, the Terrible." Ivan was a big, lovable, slobbery, goofy and obnoxious golden retriever who loved everyone to pieces. His bark was big, but all he wanted to do was to call you over to lick your face off and paint it with tons of gooey slobber while he stood on his hind legs. Once I understood this, Ivan wasn't so terrible anymore, but the name stuck anyway until I moved to another apartment complex a few months later.

Demetrius also worked at WMT in promotions. It was his hope and dream to someday get a shot at sports anchoring. He loved sports of all kinds and he often practiced a sportscast or two. I remember his calling me to a group that was looking at his latest audition tape and he asked me for advice or any pointers that might help him improve. No one had ever asked me for my opinion before. Being a student and now a very green television meteorologist, the advice and critique usually came from others for my benefit. This is where I started learning the importance of speaking life and encouragement into people and not words that tear down. Not really knowing what to say, I mentioned a couple of nitpicky things that I would work on. After the words left my mouth, I realized I was the last person in the group who should give such advice. I was a novice at television broadcasting and needed much more than jeweler's rouge to polish my delivery. But at this early stage in my broadcast career being rusty was perfectly normal. Polish comes with much time.

As far as I know, Demetrius never did find a niche in sportscasting. Years after I left Cedar Rapids, I heard that he moved on to a couple of other markets, always staying in promotions work. It may have never made a difference in his life path, but I wish now I had been more of a cheerleader and encourager by the video monitor that day.

As Dave and I deepened our friendship, he started inviting me over to his apartment to watch episodes of "Dallas" that he had videotaped on Friday night. Remember, this was 1981. Home videotape machines were the newest thing on the market. There were two formats jockeying for prominence, VHS and Beta. It doesn't matter what format it was, the newfangled machines were expensive! As I recall, Dave paid around a thousand dollars for his. He would purposefully avoid watching "Dallas" so he could fully enjoy it at a later time without the pressure of preparing the 10 PM weathercast. Doing that was even more of a challenge since we were the affiliate station that carried the program. Nonetheless, he got to be quite good at not watching. Since everyone at WMT knew he did this, everyone respected this and clammed up when he walked into a conversation about what J. R. did next, or if the Ewing family would do this or that. Watching "Dallas" in Dave's apartment became something I looked forward to every weekend. In the fall, I moved to weekday morning and noon which meant I could join Dave on Sunday evenings with a bowl of popcorn or a package of Ho-Hos and a Coke or Pepsi.

Brian Durst

By late June or early July, Brian Durst and I had begun to spend a little more time together. He lived at Park Towne Apartments a few miles from my Blake Avenue flat. I started to get to know some of Brian's neighbors in the process. It was much more like the college dorm life that I had grown comfortable with. Having friends surrounding me in a community was appealing to the point where Brian alerted me that there was an apartment waiting for a renter right down the hall from him. Despite the wonderful generosity provided by Demetrius and his wife, a garage for my car and lower monthly rent payments than Park Towne, the appeal of the Park Towne community was too strong to resist. By July, I moved the little I had into apartment N-14.

My place at Park Towne Apartments was a much better fit for me. It was just the right size, newer, and was also less than a mile away from the television studio. It was on the third floor and had a wonderful view of the western sky from both the living room and bedroom. The only disadvantage was when the bright Iowa summer sun would scream past the thin drapes and warm the place to an uncomfortable level in the early evening. Thank goodness for the free central air conditioning - that is, when it was working.

Having Brian a few doors down and on the other side of the hallway was a real gift from the Lord. Having someone familiar from college only a few doors down tempered the bouts of loneliness I felt at times. Having a very tight budget with the higher rent I was now paying made buying extras, like a vacuum, impossible. I was thankful that Brian gladly let me borrow his on a regular basis.

While I was still working weekends in the summer, there were many Saturday and Sunday evenings that we would meet for a bite to eat in between newscasts. Sometimes if there was a fair or festival going on we would meet at a pre-determined location and take in some of the merry making and taste the local flavors of good, old-fashioned Iowa farmland cooking. When I moved to weekday mornings, and when Brian would manage a weekend off, we would travel to nearby Chicago where the both of us would get our fix of urban contemporary and dance music, something that was conspicuously missing from Iowa culture.

Both of us enjoyed watching severe weather and Iowa was certainly a great place to sample it. One summer afternoon we were chasing thunderstorms in Brian's Datsun 480ZX looking for any hint of a possible tornado. Because we had Brian's sun roof removed, we stayed just outside the rain shaft all the while following the storm's movement. After a while, both of us had no idea where we were. Brian pulled to the side of the road to look at the road map to mark our location and plot our next move. While he was looking at the map, I settled back in the seat and looked directly up into the sky. Immediately, a surge of adrenalin rushed through my body as I saw that we were directly under a rotating funnel cloud. It was as if I was looking inside of a vacuum cleaner hose attachment. I could easily see inside the funnel and see the spinning motion of the cloud wall that made up the inside of it. I didn't say a word. I couldn't. I simply smacked Brian's arm and pointed directly overhead. He looked and had the same eye-popping reaction. Within seconds, he made a U-turn on the road heading back toward Cedar Rapids not paying much attention to speed restrictions on the corn-surrounded, quiet country road. I kept an eye on the funnel cloud as we fled away from it. Fortunately, it never reached for the ground.

Brian and I both shared the dream of one day working for then "Good Morning America" meteorologist, John Coleman. It was more than a dream since we waited for the time when our former professor of meteorology, Joe D'Aleo, would invite us to apply for a new concept national cable television station called, "The Weather Channel." Joe was working alongside John Coleman in Chicago in the planning stages for this new television venture. By mid-autumn 1981, Brian was offered a job helping to produce the weather segments for "Good Morning America." The operation moved to Atlanta where "The Weather Channel" would be located. Watching my Park Towne neighbor leave was difficult, but also served to remind me that I, too, had the chance to join them in time.

Lillian Bishop

My apartment on the third floor was directly above that of a wonderful lady by the name of Lillian Bishop. Because Brian lived at Park Towne Apartments, I started to get to know many of his neighbors when I still lived on Blake Avenue. They would often sit under a shady tree enjoying the summer breezes together. It was in this way that I met Lillian.

She was a petite woman whose joyful countenance was contagious. A retired schoolteacher from Ottumwa, Iowa, Lillian made everyone feel like they were special. I'm certain that is the way she viewed everyone she met.

When I moved to Park Towne in July, she went out of her way to embrace me as an integral part of the special community in our building. It didn't take me long to see that she was instrumental in strengthening the family-like bonds that existed there. But for me, it was her maternal guidance that filled a gap for which my mother in New Bedford will be forever grateful. She became a "proxy-Mom," so-to-speak.

Several memories that stand out always give me a smile. The kind of smile you give yourself when you realize just how rich God has made your life. Such was the hot Iowa day when I saw Lillian sitting in that shady spot near the front entrance of our apartment building. She was there in her portable lawn chair along with three or four others. Despite the heat, they looked perfectly content to enjoy each other's company. But I was bothered that they must be getting uncomfortably warm. It was 95 degrees and there wasn't much of a breeze blowing. I looked in my freezer and found a half gallon of unopened vanilla ice cream. Within minutes, I was carrying bowls of unsolicited ice cream drizzled with chocolate sauce on a makeshift tray down two flights of stairs. They were all delighted with my gesture. For a few minutes, I joined them in their light conversation as we all gobbled up the ice cream. Not knowing how they tolerated the heat so well, I excused myself and went back into my apartment where the central air at least took the edge off of the heat.

Then there were the days when I drifted by her open door and she could sense that something was wrong. Lillian never let me get away with a simple wave as I walked past. She insisted that I come in for a visit. Genuinely interested in what was going on in my life, she was always asking about Sally, my parents, and people I was close to at the station. Just like the proxy mother she was to me, she also gave me the room I needed to comfortably share my heart when it was heavy. Sometimes it was missing Sally, who was about to begin her senior year at Lyndon State College. Other times it might have been feeling discouraged from a not-so-stellar weathercast on television. In every case, she was a powerful cheerleader and reminded me how special I was to everyone around me. There wasn't a single visit to the apartment below mine where I didn't walk out with a new outlook on life.

Lillian's love for people was driven by something deep. The evidence for this is forever etched in my mind by a scene I witnessed frequently when passing by her open apartment door. There were many instances when I walked by quietly without her knowing it. On those days, she would be sitting quietly by the window in her favorite chair with a book on her lap that was so big that it seemed to dwarf her small frame. It was her big-print Bible. It is one of my favorite images to recall because of the unmistakable look of inner peace she radiated. There was something reassuring about having someone one floor below me that had a powerful connection to God. It was as if I benefited from the overflow of a blessing. Indeed, that was the case since I carry that image with me today with perfect clarity as if I had walked by her door yesterday.

More then twenty years after leaving Cedar Rapids and after losing track of where Lillian had moved to, I was able to locate where she was living. After calling the listed number and leaving several messages on her answering machine, we finally reconnected. Exchanging news was such a treat. My true motive, though, was to tell her about the influence she had on my life. I wanted her to know how much her quiet, unknowing witness inspired me in ways she could have never imagined.

A Visit From Bob

As busy as life was in the first summer away from the city I called home, there were still plenty of moments during which loneliness crept back in. In between visits from Sally and my handful of quick, two-day trips to visit with her and her family in Cleveland, visitors were noticeably absent. My father was still working in the restaurant business, and getting away for a trip to Iowa with my mother was a tall order. Not being seasoned fliers, a flight to Cedar Rapids from Boston would have given them both ulcers from all the connections that they would have needed to make, not to mention the prohibitively high price of an airline ticket to a small town in Iowa.

Throughout the summer Bob Gilmore would stay in touch with me. Being a radiophile and deeply interested in television broadcasts as well, he was excited about my new role at WMT-AM-FM and TV and called for updates on how things were going. Well before Sally drove me to Iowa, Bob talked about the possibility of driving out to visit me there. I knew Bob would drive a few hours north of his Connecticut home to visit with me while at Lyndon

State, but would he really drive over 24 hours west? That was answered when he called me in the middle of the summer and announced his intention to drive the furthest west he had ever driven.

After a brief visit to Wisconsin before coming to Iowa, Bob arrived on the last Wednesday in July. True to his form, he brought his portable recording equipment to sample local radio stations along the way. I would have been surprised and even a little disappointed had he not.

In addition to showing him the studios of WMT and him coming in with me for some of my on-air shifts, we also went north to a small water slide park that I had heard about from someone. It was in Waverly, Iowa, not far from the television and radio tower farm for a lot of the stations in the area. Bob was awestruck at how long and lean the towers were and how it contrasted against an absolutely flat horizon. The Midwest is home to many of the tallest television towers in the United States, most of them well over a thousand feet tall. The nearby water slide park was perfect for the warm summer evening when we took the one hour drive north from Cedar Rapids. We stayed there until well past sunset getting waterlogged. In fact, they probably had to kick us out at closing time.

Bob's visit to Iowa was an important one in so many dimensions. He was my only visitor from New England. That was a welcomed tonic to my intense loneliness. More importantly, it escorted an already strong bond of friendship to a new level knowing that someone would craft their summer vacation to drive halfway across the country to spend some time with me. That blessing went a long way to bringing peace to the rest of my summer as I listened to the corn grow.

Richard

Richard lived by himself on the south side of our Park Towne apartment building. He always seemed like a man that was comfortable in his own skin. I suspect he was probably somewhat past retirement age as he always seemed to be around. Just like everyone else, Richard adopted me into the community. While I sensed he got a kick out of having a local television personality living in the same building as he did, there was no special treatment beyond the usual kindness given to everyone. He was a small-framed man with an energetic walk. He often wore a dark green tuque, a type of knitted hat, any time that it was cool, and he spoke with slight speech impediment that made his voice unmistakable.

One of the things I remember Richard for was his unending invitation to take me out to the local Wendy's, only a block or so away from our building, for a "Frosty." I had never heard of them at the time having worked at McDonald's for six years while in high school and college. I knew everything there was to know about McDonald's, but I drew a blank when it came to any other fast food menus. Richard insisted that a Frosty was the ultimate treat. Despite my turning him down continually, he persisted with his kind invitations.

I don't remember when it was that I finally accepted his invitation, but one day I did. He was like a kid leading another kid to a secret stash of candy bars. He was thrilled that he would introduce me to the Frosty. This gave us the chance to talk beyond usual pleasantries and get to know each other on a deeper level.

Somehow, the topic turned to life's regrets. For most twenty-two year olds, I suspect the majority of them would be in the college era and this certainly was the case for me. He listened patiently as I shared some of those events. He must have sensed that I was having a difficult time forgiving myself. It did not take long for Richard to stop me after a little while to remind me that God had provided the forgiveness I needed to move forward. He encouraged me to live in that forgiveness so that I could look ahead with more confidence. He was so right not once but twice. First, that I could find and live in God's forgiveness, and second, that a Wendy's Frosty was a tasty treat.

That was my first Frosty ever. My next one would not come for a very long time. Twenty-six years and three cities later, the dean of Cleveland television weather, Dick Goddard, offered to buy me a Frosty during a dinner run after the six o'clock news. I immediately thought of the first Richard to buy me a Frosty. It was only fitting to have another kind soul by the name of Richard buy me my second.

After two freebies, I have since paid for my own.

A Fork In The Road

The winter winds began to whip across the plains. There was snow and blowing snow and some bitterly cold outbreaks. At the end of a long work week, Dave and I scratched our heads as we looked at a typical midwest arctic outbreak. Winter warnings and talk of ground blizzards from blowing snow was enough to mean that both Dave and I would be taking shifts that had us doing weather cut-ins beginning at the end of the ten o'clock newscast that Friday night with plans to go well into Saturday as needed. As the night went on, it was apparent that nothing would happen. Finally just after sunrise Saturday morning when the skeleton crew was getting very punchy from sleep deprivation, we received a welcomed dismissal from our post.

Not long after, my former Lyndon State College professor, Joe D'Aleo, called me with the invitation I was hoping and praying for. The idea of an all-weather cable station was well beyond conceived and had a planned birthdate sometime in the spring. Joe invited me to be on the launch team.

The ink on my three-year contract with WMT-TV, whose call letters changed to KGAN-TV in October, had barely dried. The only provision for an early release was a "top-twenty out." In other words, I could leave for any station that made me an employment offer in a city located in any top-twenty television market. While "The Weather Channel" was going to be a national cable television station, the actual facility would be in Atlanta, Georgia, which qualified it as a top-twenty market. Technically, the contract did not state that the employer had to be a local television station.

Feeling sheepish about exercising my option so soon after arriving in Iowa, I told Bob Jackson, the news director, about the offer and that I was seriously considering it. What happened next surprised me the most. After a day or two of asking me to wait before rendering my decision, management came back and matched "The Weather Channel" offer and even added a few other incentives. A miniature bidding war broke out between KGAN and TWC. After a few volleys back and forth, KGAN hit their ceiling and a tough decision hung in the balance. When the rubber met the road it was one question from my brother-in-law that cleared any doubt that I had.

"Can you envision yourself remaining in Cedar Rapids for the rest of your broadcast weather career?"

As charming as life could be in the plains, I knew it was time to move on. The very next day, I told Bob Jackson that I had accepted the offer from "The Weather Channel." I guess I wasn't sure what Bob's reaction would be but, to my relief, he surprised me with a warm and firm handshake and a genuine congratulatory smile. As much as he tried to keep me at KGAN, he was also equally happy for the next adventure in my career. I agreed to stay through the important February ratings period. That amounted to about a month and a half.

At first, it seemed like ample time to get all of my affairs in order. How quickly I forgot how time-consuming a move could be. I had a great deal of help in moving to Iowa. Preparing for a move to Atlanta was a solo affair and seemed overwhelming at times. But

God graciously met me in some wonderful ways.

KGAN was quick to locate and hire my replacement, a gentleman by the name of Don Chilo who went by an on-air name of Don Keith. Don needed a place to move to, and I needed to find someone to rent my apartment or face paying for the rest of my one-year agreement.

Wanting a fresh start in Atlanta, I sold or gave away everything that I could not fit into my 1981 Ford Mustang. Some co-workers took my bed and the little furniture I had. I gave Dave Towne my philodendron plant that my mother had given me from a clipping of the one she had in my boyhood home. (Dave tells me that he still has it and it has thrived for more than two decades!) By my final week in Iowa I was living out of a suitcase in a totally empty apartment with many of my belongings already packed in the Mustang.

Friday, February 26, 1982. It was my last day at KGAN. Aside from a now empty apartment, the work day was like any other day. I was up at four o'clock and arrived at the station while the "test pattern" was still on (regular programming did not begin until "CBS Sunrise" at 6:30 AM). Between the morning weather cut-ins and the noon weathercast, I was busy with people swinging by the office to say goodbye. Thankfully, the weather was quiet and afforded me the time to spend with some of the people who made the first eight months of my television career special. Dave and a few others in the newsroom suggested that we have a short send-off lunch at a local eatery right after the noon newscast and just before I began my two-day drive to Georgia. It sounded like a great way to end my first professional tenure.

But my enthusiasm would quickly turn to frustration after walking out of the KGAN studios for the last time as an employee. My overstuffed Mustang had two flat tires. I assumed that the weight of what I was bringing with me was too much for a small, sporty car to handle. Even if I was able to get the tires fixed, the thought of driving over a thousand miles with my belongings stuffed under pressure like a croissant dough tube made me second-guess the success of reaching my destination. One of my co-workers filled my tires with enough air so that I could drive it to a service station near the restaurant to which my friends were taking me. Even as I ate a delightful lunch and enjoyed being with my friends, I prayed.

After lunch, the mechanic had some good news. He could find nothing wrong with the tires at all. It appeared as though a prankster had let the air out of them. The mechanic assured me that, while my Mustang had only enough room left for one driver, my trip should be uneventful.

At three o'clock in the afternoon, Cedar Rapids was in my rear view mirror. I was leaving behind many special people, but I was taking all of the investments they had made in my life. Those were investments that are still paying dividends today.

After driving as long as I could on the first leg of my journey southeast, my eyelids demanded a place to sleep after the adrenalin of excitement wore off. It was midnight when I finally pulled into a motel in Vincennes, Indiana. I was already missing my friends and the cold, dark air and unfamiliar town did nothing but amplify that sensation. Part of me wanted to drive back to Iowa, but I knew that it would be a while before I returned, and only as a visitor.

Chapter 5

No Longer A Dream

Less than twenty-four hours after leaving Iowa, the enormity of the change sank in when I stopped into a Nashville McDonald's for lunch on my final leg to Atlanta. After several hours of driving in freezing rain, I was tired from the mental strain of having to remain mentally acute on the icy roads. I was ready for a fast meal. The cashier greeted me with the thickest southern drawl I had ever personally encountered in my life. It took my brain an extra second to realize that she was speaking English. I was in the deep south for the first time in my life. Culture shock set in.

By late Saturday afternoon, I arrived at my new apartment in the same complex as one of my college friends, Nick Gregory, who worked as one of the meteorologists on staff at CNN. It was Nick who arranged that for me. The apartment was barren and cool, and the cold rain and bleak skies didn't do anything to make me feel like I was welcome. Unfortunately, Nick was on vacation in New York so I had no company as I unstuffed the Mustang and moved all of my boxes into the living room. At least by the time I was done, the apartment had warmed. Turning on all the lights also helped to chase the gloom out of my new digs. I had less than two days to arrange for some temporary furniture and to become familiar with Atlanta before heading in for my first day of work at a national cable television network that did not even exist yet. I stared out of the sliding glass door and beyond the deck which overlooked a beautiful Georgia pine forest. The door was not even open and I could smell its fragrance. It was finally feeling a little more like my new home.

On Monday, March 1, 1982, the largest group of broadcast and support meteorologists outside of a professional conference assembled in a large room which would eventually become the data hub of "The Weather Channel." Swimming against the strong current of nearly every industry soothsayer, we began putting the pieces in place for a coast-to-coast, non-stop weathercast. It was somewhat difficult to fathom that an entire floor of an office building still buzzing with construction workers and whose floors were still slippery with construction dust was only 62 days away from launching. No one could envision it. The only person who might have had an idea was the mind behind the dream of a national cable television station devoted to around-the-clock weather coverage.

There was more than one dream though. At the very least, a second one was riding on the coat tails of the first. Little did I know that mine would become a reality in a very special way.

John Coleman

During my junior year in high school, the ABC morning program, "Good Morning America," made its big debut splash. It was different. That difference set them apart from NBC's "Today Show." Once a fan of NBC news anchor Frank Blair presenting a synopsis of the nation's weather, my attention was quickly drawn to someone who not only made weather sound irresistible, but took those nuggets of time to be America's early morning professor in the process. There wasn't a single morning that I would miss John

Coleman's weathercasts beamed to New York from his Chicago studio. With school starting at just before eight, I could only grab his first weather segment at 7:12 A.M. most days. When I was lucky enough to have a ride to school, I could sometimes squeak in the second at the bottom of the hour. It was clear that he had an intense passion for weather and more importantly had a dimension of joy and fun that was addictive.

While attending Lyndon State College, mornings were a bit less rushed. Breakfast was always an important meal at home and that carried over to my college days where I missed no more than one or two breakfasts in four years. Either before the dining hall opened or after fueling our bodies for a day of academics, many meteorology students would meet in the student lounges to see what John had up his sleeve that day. Pulling out weather maps from thin air, jumping and waltzing around a weather set that seemed enormous, and always teaching something new in his "weather extra" segment kept all of us glued to "Good Morning America" every weekday morning. One of those fellow classmates was Nick Gregory from New York City. Nick and I regularly imitated John's deliberate articulation of the sponsors like, "The Bell System," and "Nabisco." It was an imitation of endearment.

I have always been a proponent of positive projection, that is, "visioncasting," not in a meteorological sense but in the way one daydreams about setting and reaching professional and personal goals. After watching the likes of Don Kent, Bruce Schwoegler and John Ghiorse delivering nightly weathercasts when I was a young boy in southern New England, I began imitating them. With whatever props that I could find, I would imitate them, delivering weathercasts without an audience. Eventually, a room in our Sutton Street basement slowly evolved into a piecemeal weather office with all-band radios to pick up transcribed weather broadcasts out of Boston's Logan Airport, NOAA weather radios, a very sensitive AM radio whose antenna actually wrapped around the roofline to tune into other distant cities, and an erasable weather map that my sister made me for Christmas one year.

Every afternoon after school, I invariably spent time seeing myself one day delivering weather by going through the motions of preparing and delivering forecasts to my audience, the furnace and stairwell.

Yearning for a more legitimate audience, I was able to convince the New Bedford High School headmaster to allow me to deliver a daily weather forecast during morning announcements to the student body, which numbered around three thousand. Temporarily satisfying, it wasn't enough and I eventually began my radio career on WBSM at age 15. I loved radio and this only fueled my aspiration to one day do the same on television.

Something happened in 1976. After watching John Coleman spin his brand of covering national weather, my visioncasting began to drift. While I used to like watching NBC newscaster Frank Blair broad brush the morning national weather, John brought something new to the table. Trained in meteorology, he broke free from the old, mundane format of covering national weather with a style that was not only educational but entertaining. Even before meeting Nick Gregory in college, I would occasionally try to deliver a national weathercast to my steadfast audience, the furnace and stairwell, ending with John's standard cue.

"That's the national weather. Now your local forecast."

What is the chance that a curly-haired, weather-crazy kid from New Bedford, Massachusetts could ever rise to the rank of television meteorologist on a national network? Next to nothing, that is, until I thought of all the encouragement I received up to that point, starting with my fifth grade teacher, my parents and my Uncle Arthur. God provided so much encouragement through so many people that the only limits I would encounter would be the ones that I set myself.

While certainly enjoying my first assignment at WMT-TV, I would still find my mind wandering about my professional journey ahead. I loved walking places from my apartment and as the days began to cool in September, my walks became more frequent. It was the perfect antidote to the unusual sense of loneliness I felt which stemmed from the oddity of not heading to a class or a college campus. For virtually all of my life up to that point, September meant school, books, friends, classes, and cooler weather. The only element that followed me to Cedar Rapids was the cooler weather. There were no schools to head to, no books to buy, all of my friends were now scattered across the country, and the only class to which I now belonged was the working one. Going for long walks helped me to find sensible places for the new pieces of life's jigsaw puzzle.

During those walks, I tried to picture myself two, five, and ten years from that moment and I'd invariably come back to the same wild grab at the stars. It ended with the same sentences - "That's the national weather! Now your local forecast."

Only months later, I found myself in Atlanta surrounded by over five dozen meteorologists, some of whom I had watched on television growing up. Together, we were standing on the precipice of making national television history.

The highlight was having as my boss the one figure I enjoyed watching and emulating the most, John Coleman. Placing John on such a lofty pedestal for so long did me no favors in that it made my initial meetings with him intimidating. His booming bass voice was even more resonant in person. He went from being my favorite television meteorologist to my boss and mentor.

I was twenty-two years old and still quite impressionable. Like others in the early stage of a television career, my tendency was to try to pattern my style after someone I admired. Much to the irritation of a few of my new co-workers, my inclination to pattern my on-air performance after John's GMA style was far from subtle. I couldn't have cared less about scoring brownie points. Rather, it was a style I was comfortable wearing until my own personality began to slowly add a unique flavor to a style John owned.

There was much work to be done before the launch date just two months away. Construction ramped up. By late March the studio was completed and we began going through mock weather blocks that were either thirty or sixty minutes in length. The technical and art departments were busy creating and tweaking the key maps that would become the signature look of TWC in its first half decade of operation. The technology was cutting edge. Some of it developed before our eyes as the needs dictated inventions such as the "Weather Star" unit that delivered location specific forecasts simultaneously to all the cable markets we would serve, all delivered by satellite. Television weather would never look the same.

Assigning the schedule for 64 meteorologists must have been a challenge for management. Everyone hoped for a high visibility slot and everyone held their breath when the assignments were published in mid-April. I truly had no idea where I would be positioned. I had a hunch it would be during the morning drive time since that is what I was last doing at KGAN-TV. What I discovered surprised me. I was being assigned to afternoons and early evenings. Everyone's days off floated every few weeks to give everyone the chance to have weekends off. This was only the "first draft" and might be tweaked before our actual on-air launch sometime during the NAB (National Association of Broadcasters) convention in Las Vegas in early May.

By late April, the start date and time was announced. TWC's debut broadcast from Atlanta would follow a live ceremony from Las Vegas. Dual switches, one in Las Vegas and one in Atlanta, would be thrown at 8 P.M. Eastern on Sunday, May 2, 1982. While I was not initially on the anchor team that would carry the first thirty minute block, I was thrilled to have a block later that evening.

With less than one week before the network's debut to the nation the final adjustment to the on-air schedule was released. There were changes. Big changes. I was no longer on the third anchor team. A rush of adrenalin surged through me as a looked again and again to make sure what I was reading was real. The debut anchor team for the very first thirty minute block was now scheduled to be Bruce Edwards (Kalinowski) and me. Practice shows that final week took on extra meaning. If I was going to help anchor the very first block on TWC's debut broadcast, I wanted to be as polished as I could be.

On Sunday, May 2, 1981, the second floor office on Mt. Wilkinson Parkway was buzzing with last minute preparations. Just a little before eight o'clock, Bruce and I were in place. Quite honestly I can't remember what we were saying to each other or even what I was thinking beyond how I would address the nation when we went on the air. Bruce was doing the same. Our chatter was minimal as we waited for our cue, two buttons simultaneously pushed from Las Vegas and Atlanta that would roll the first station I.D.

It was eight o'clock. The ceremonial buttons were pushed and the animated logo flew in. Bruce was the lead anchor so he began and I followed.

"And good evening America. Welcome to 'The Weather Channel,' the non-ending, weather telethon. I'm Bruce Edwards. Glad to be with you this evening."

"And I'm André Bernier. Glad you could join us from wherever you are viewing across the country. Hello, everybody."

"We were the fortunate pair that happened by the luck of the draw to choose this premiere showing of 'The Weather Channel'... and without any further ado, let's get to the weather happenings tonight."

The "weather telethon," as Bruce dubbed it, had just begun. It did not hit me until after I drove back to my apartment in nearby

Marietta after midnight that I had just received a special gift. The dream that my Creator implanted deep in my soul, that came into sharp focus while watching "Good Morning America" in 1975, had come to pass only seven years later thanks to the man I watched who was now my boss. That crazy dream wasn't so crazy after all. At age twenty-two, I was delivering weathercasts to a national television audience. It took years for me to be able to wrap my mind around this gift. Even now, almost thirty years later, I marvel at the world's instant access to the very first minute of TWC's broadcast history with a simple click of a mouse on YouTube. Bruce and I might have been even more nervous knowing just how huge this moment in cable history would turn out to be.

John was a perfectionist. His segments on GMA proved that time and time again. When it came to molding and tweaking a wild, abstract idea into reality, a national cable network, he was hands-on in every aspect. Critics wanted him to delegate more of the day-to-day operations but he had too much of himself invested in the end product to be able to do that. Forever with a diet Tab in his hand, we would see him bopping into virtually every office almost every day.

For the first year, John reviewed and critiqued our performance both collectively and individually. Most everyone found these critiques more than just a little unnerving. While I, too, was nervous about each scheduled critique, I was also excited about them. We would watch a recent thirty minute block together after which the pause before John spoke felt like I was waiting for Simon Cowell to tell me what he really thought about my singing. The honesty was brutal but fair. In hindsight, I think he was just a little easier on me compared to my co-workers. Perhaps it was because he saw the young kid who was always trying to emulate him.

A few years later, circumstances arose that forced John to leave the national network that was his dream, but not before walking a mile out of his way to help me pave a road from a crazy dream to history-making reality.

Don Buser

After a year on evenings, TWC brass thought my on-air energy level might be better suited for morning drive time. They gave me an option to move to a morning slot that began at 6:00 A.M. The notion appealed to me since I was used to getting up early for most of my life. My father routinely awoke, without an alarm clock, at four o'clock to head to the Diner Deluxe that he owned and operated. My mother was up by five and everyone was up and having breakfast at six. The first year on evenings at TWC seemed out of sync with what I was used to for so long. With morning drive time becoming more important on national cable, I took them up on the offer.

I recently came across a letter that my mother sent just before the switch to mornings soon after Easter weekend in 1983. In it, she celebrated the move since she knew it would be more in sync with my tendency to be more of a morning person but warned me to be vigilant against depriving myself of a good night's rest.

Just as the move from weekday mornings to weekday evenings at WJW-TV in Cleveland in 2007 meant working with an entirely new crew, the same held true back in 1983. We were all hired together in March of 1982, but after the schedule was decided upon I would hardly ever get to see about half of the on-air staff unless they had arranged a shift swap.

While coffee was flowing fast, the morning crew had a natural energetic temperament that probably didn't need the extra caffeine. Morning viewers of TWC welcomed Bill Schubert, Brian Durst (my former college classmate), Mark Mancuso, Bill Keneely, and Don Buser into their kitchens and living rooms. Watching the sunrise felt more natural. In each of our longer breaks, many of us would wander one building south to a delightful breakfast nook located on the ground floor of that office building. While I missed the crew from evenings, my friendships with the morning crew seemed to grow quickly.

Somehow, a special friendship developed between an unlikely pair. I was a die-hard New Englander. Don Buser had the thickest Mississippi accent I had ever heard on or off television. I liked linguiça and he liked grits. I liked snow and cold. He liked heat and humidity. But just like Laurel and Hardy, there was a quirky chemistry between us. Incurably joyful and optimistic, Don's charm was natural and genuine.

We were paired up together in the studio at least a half-dozen times every week, and the contrast between a northerner and a southerner was something with which we had a great deal of liberty to have unbridled fun during our segments. I can still clearly see one of the graphics we used going into commercial breaks. It was a photo I snapped at an I-75 interchange. The overhead sign had traffic for I-75 north going right and for I-75 south going left. Years before Photoshop was ever invented, our art department electronically manipulated the photo, replacing the cities listed so that the sign read "Bernier" on the right and "Buser" on the left.

In between blocks, Don was frequently relaxing in the briefing room with a tumbler of coffee and a doughnut. He did this frequently at the expense of what might be considered a more "normal" breakfast or lunch. Eventually, he saw a doctor about the increasing frequency with which he had severe headaches. After some probing, the doctor asked him was his diet was like and discovered that a large measure of his food intake consisted of doughnuts and sweetened coffee. After some quick adjustments to what he was eating and drinking, something we all noticed almost immediately, the headaches disappeared.

When we had some free time, the casual chats that Don and I enjoyed included far more than the usual surface pleasantries. By this time my then fiancée and I had an interest in spiritual matters, Don would amaze us with his Biblical knowledge. He never once used the knowledge as a prideful tool but rather liberally shared what he knew if he sensed there was interest. Additionally, he bandied in such a way that made what can be a confusing subject relevant and fascinating.

He was particularly fascinated with Dr. John Thomas who, in the 19th century, moved from England to America. After being nearly shipwrecked in the process, Dr. Thomas vowed to find the truth about life's journey and God through intense, personal study in God's Word. Eventually, those who embraced his quest to live with the zeal and focus of the first-century church became known as the Christadelphians. While Don was not a Christadelphian, he thought well of them and embraced their quest for the truth of the Bible and not the traditions of men.

It was an interesting period spiritually. In discussing the Bible with Sally, I encouraged her to read the Scriptures for herself with regard to eschatology (study of end times). Always up for a challenge, the first book of the Bible she ever read was Revelation. Few people who have read Scriptures for the first time can say that they started with such a symbolically-driven book.

Lane Roberts, another on-camera meteorologist, also noticed our spiritual interests. Lane was active in the church that he and his wife attended and extended a number of invitations to join them for Sunday services. Sally and I did join them a couple of times, but because they lived 45 minutes away, it was difficult to consider making that a home church.

We did visit a number of churches that were closer. While some were interesting, most were a difficult fit for someone like me who had a religious background that was structured and liturgical. Sally had virtually no background for a reference, but the charismatic elements raised more questions than the ones she had.

Finally, working on Sunday mornings while having to cycle through the on-camera schedule made finding a church home a non-reality.

Despite not being a regular church attender, a spiritual germination was taking place. I now see the wisdom in living out the Bible's precepts every day since speaking with Don while at work was where I was able to grow as a Christian the most during my three years in Atlanta.

Don and his wife, "Dee," made their beautiful north Georgia home an open base in which all of us at TWC felt right at home. Pool parties, barbeques, picnics and casual drop-ins for lemonade and iced tea were commonplace. Don and Dee even helped to organize enough people to start our own bowling league. TWC employees took up more than a dozen lanes every week. We took joy in not only working together but playing together as well.

During the formative stages of our bowling league, I was able to convince Sally, Brian Durst and one of our artists to call our team the "Woollybear Watchers" after Vermilion, Ohio's gigantic yearly autumn festival that looks to the woolly bear caterpillar for the winter forecast. I wrote to Dick Goddard, Cleveland weather icon, to ask him if he would supply us with woolly bear tee shirts for our team. Not only did he send tee shirts, but a wide variety of paraphernalia related to the woolly bear festival. Not knowing that he had become a TWC junkie, he was thrilled to send us our team colors and to have a point of contact at his favorite cable channel. Little did I know that the new friendship would one day lead to a chance to work with him, side-by-side.

The time came when I would move on from the national cable station, but Don and I remained in close contact. We even exchanged visits a number of times with Don flying north to brave the deep chill of Minnesota and me flying back south to Atlanta where it always felt like I was coming home when staying at their house.

Don stayed true to his love for warm weather. After leaving TWC, he moved to West Palm Beach and traded his suits and ties for polo shirts. In recent years, our phone calls continue to be colored by his same deep desire to grow in God's Word. Don is forever reaching for the kind of wisdom that the world cannot offer. I am thrilled to know that some of that wisdom rubbed off on me as we walked together for a season.

If You Can't Stand The Heat

Early in my career, one of my desires was to find my way back to New England. Atlanta was beautiful, especially in the spring. Winters were delightfully easy. On the other hand, summers were difficult for someone used to cooling Atlantic sea breezes and occasional cool, dry days to break up the summer heat. Summers were long, hot and humid. The sun was so intense for so long that in late September when we had our first totally cloudy day, all of the local newscasts occupied the first ten minutes with stories related to the lack of sunshine with sighs of relief and celebration. It was likely the oddest thing I had ever seen in Atlanta.

After a couple of years, the initial glow of being on national television faded. A couple of us, including Don, tried to figure out the level of hyper-experience a TWC on-camera meteorologist (OCM) was getting. We calculated the number of daily minutes each spent actually on the air and were amazed. For every year we worked at "The Weather Channel," each OCM accrued as much time on the air as a local market television meteorologist would take seven years to accumulate. On an active weather day, there was enough variety and change around the country to make things interesting and lively. Conversely on the days when the whole country was largely quiet and sunny, working five on-air blocks felt about as exciting as presenting a three-hour lecture on the migration habits of the Black-tailed Godwit.

I began to miss the challenge of the local forecast and began to casually look for other opportunities. Denver's powerhouse, KUSA-TV, contacted me about a weekday morning position in which they thought I would be a good fit. I loved the thought of being close to mountains and, being a skier, relished the thought of so many ski areas within driving distance. I agreed to explore this possibility and they flew me out to meet with their weather team and to watch several days worth of newscasts. It was a stunning operation and I enjoyed the thought of living in the Rockies. Legendary weather icons, Stormy Rottman and Bill Kuster, made me feel like I was already on their payroll. I flew home hoping that they would make an offer while in the same breath pondered the complications of a possible long distance engagement with Sally.

A week later they called me and offered me the job but there was one small problem. As much as I loved Colorado, the salary was less than what I was making at TWC. The difference was only three thousand dollars. After several conversations with KUSA brass, it was clear that they were either not able or not willing to match my salary. Soaked in disappointment, I turned the offer down. God had a different plan.

Early in my career at TWC, I developed a casual relationship with Lee Giles, a news director at Indianapolis' powerhouse station, WISH-TV. Lee was kind enough to continually encourage me in evaluating my work even though he had no position open. During a vacation and road trip back to Iowa to visit Dave Towne and Lillian Bishop, I stopped in Indy to see Lee. It was nice matching the face to the voice that had showed me so much kindness, never once refusing my many calls.

A few years later, Lee called me to ask if I would be interested in a created position for a new, weekday morning newscast. I could easily picture myself in Indianapolis. Perhaps it was because I had grown fond of the rural landscape in Iowa since the stunning megalopolis was neatly surrounded by miles and miles of amazing farmland. It was equally impressive that many television icons passed through Indianapolis such as NBC's Jane Pauley, a young journalism graduate that Lee Giles hired in 1972 before her ascent to the "Today Show." But as alluring as Indianapolis was, something deep inside told me that I needed to forgo a career stop in the breadbasket of Indiana.

Years later, Lee told me that my decision was a good one since their first attempt at breaking into the market with a morning newscast did not succeed. In just a few years, I would have been looking for work. In hindsight, that "something deep inside" was nothing less than God's Spirit protecting my footsteps. I'm glad that I was able to hear His voice.

Eventually, Sally received an offer from the NBC affiliate in Minneapolis. I took a deep breath and, with youthful confidence, packed my bags and put Atlanta in my rearview mirror, leaving behind a place where I was able to fulfill a dream and career goal. It was only three-and-a-half years after its humble beginning, but "The Weather Channel" wasn't the same place that it was in March of 1982. So much had changed, aside from a long struggle to become profitable. Much of the joy and passion that once filled my cup was now nearly exhausted. I was weary of the heat and tired of grits, so heading to the North Wood was appealing. It was time. Most of all, I had a sense of peace.

Chapter 6

Northbound

The apartment was empty again. My foot was barely healed from laser surgery to remove several stubborn plantar warts as I stuffed in the car the last of my belongings beyond that which was being ferried north by moving van. It was time to leave.

In the quiet solitude, I was moved by the Spirit of God to praise Him for all he had richly given to me in Atlanta and then to raise my hands and pronounce a blessing on all future occupants who would call this place home. Sensing His pleasure with my praise and request, I said goodbye to Georgia and never looked back. It was an unusual sentiment in that, with every other professional move I had in my career, I had a period of six to twelve months of second-guessing and yearning for the familiar things left behind. Not so with Georgia.

Before joining my bride-to-be in Minnesota, I planned on driving up the east coast to New England to visit with my family for a few days. There was one major problem. It was Gloria. Gloria was doing everything possible to get in the way of my plan.

Both Interstates 85 and 95 had become much busier than normal. In some cases, it was a parking lot. Gloria, a powerful east coast hurricane, was wreaking havoc in the Carolinas and headed for New England. Rather than placing myself in the middle of a traffic jam on the hurricane evacuation routes, I elected to drive north and to spend the night in Cleveland. It would pad enough time for Gloria to move out of the way. I would actually save time by crafting the drive into two twelve-hour legs.

Driving the second leg felt a little like driving into a known battle zone. As the sun set, I began to pull in WBZ-AM in Boston which devoted its entire coverage to non-stop weather updates and emergency information. Gloria had made landfall along the Connecticut shoreline at lunchtime and was moving through New Hampshire and Maine in the afternoon. The most dramatic change in landscape came in the last hour of my drive toward New Bedford. Powerful winds earlier in the day caused widespread power outages and by the time I reached New Bedford, the only lights I saw were from cars on the littered streets and highways. I can't remember seeing Sutton Street, or any street for that matter, looking so black.

While damage to my childhood home was minimal, it would take over a week for power to be restored to that part of New Bedford. The joy of seeing family was tempered by the unusual adventure of operating in an Amish lifestyle. The familiar background hum of anything electrical was absent. I can remember sitting down at a desk in the basement by candlelight writing in my journal about the sound of silence being so foreign. I imagined that the sights and sounds of a single family home were just like this over a hundred years ago. I could not ignore my own thoughts, something that is so easy to do today with voluminous distractions which prevent deep thought and meditation. As inconvenient as it may have been, there was a part of me that enjoyed it.

Pockets of life began to spring up as power was restored street-by-street, but when it was time for me to start heading west, Sutton Street was still very dark at night. I hated leaving before a sense of normalcy returned to my parents' lives, but a new chapter in a new state needed to begin. My drive to Minnesota would be a two-day affair. Once again, Cleveland would be my oasis.

On the second day of my drive west, nightfall greeted me in Wisconsin as I pressed northwest on Interstate 94. Despite being determined to arrive in Minneapolis early, it looked like I would be lucky to cross the Wisconsin-Minnesota border at midnight.

The wind had become noticeably colder and gustier as the night wore on. I thought it was odd that I was reaching for the car heat. The last time I remembered flicking it on was in late February in Atlanta. At midnight, nearly to the second, I passed the sign that read, "Welcome to Minnesota." Only minutes later, a foreign substance was streaking across my headlights. It didn't take me long to realize that I was driving through a snow shower. Laughter was my only response. Running into a welcoming committee of snowflakes in the minutes-old month of October was more than humorous. I saw it as an interesting omen.

Initially, I jumped on board as on-air talent and consultant at WWTC-AM. After a number of format changes trying to attract an audience in the dwindling world of AM radio, the owners decided to try a format that no other commercial AM radio station had ever attempted - all weather, all the time. Essentially, it was an attempt to replicate the television popularity of "The Weather Channel" in the radio world. If it was going to work in any market, it had a chance in a place like Minneapolis where the weather was constantly changing and went through seasonal extremes.

Unfortunately, the format was too rigidly structured and far too repetitive. Persistent suggestions to add personality and flavor to the format by adding live elements and live phone calls during severe weather events fell on deaf ears. Without something fresh to draw listeners on a regular basis, the format was slipping into a version of NOAA weather radio with commercials. What might have become an interesting format was going to die on the vine within a year. It gave me enough time to wiggle my way into Northwest Airline as a trans-Atlantic flight meteorologist in their Minneapolis flight operations center.

While I was able to enjoy some freelance, on-air fill-in at KARE-11 where Sally worked, diving into the world of commercial aviation full time was a fascinating change of pace from the broadcast news world. Northwest Airline was famous for its development of turbulence forecasting and I was now working among the meteorologists who pioneered that research. It was not uncommon for other major carriers to ask air traffic control where the "red tail" was going since they wanted to follow Northwest's track knowing full well it would lead to the smoothest flight.

While there was an element of forecasting that dealt with surface conditions, the vast majority of our energy went into upper wind forecasts, taking advantage of strong tailwinds and avoiding strong headwinds. The annual fuel savings to the company made our department invaluable.

Pete Schenck

The paradigm shift necessary to go from broadcast meteorology to aviation meteorology was no small task. While the changeover did not diminish the significance of a very important function, my audience no longer consisted of millions of Americans but instead several hundred pilots and dispatchers. Transitioning from mass media to computer text messages also took a great deal of adjusting.

Another adjustment I had to get used to was that there was virtually no margin for shortcutting. Every product that we cranked out hourly and daily was used by either a pilot or dispatcher somewhere. I learned that the best thing that we could hope for in order to stay ahead of the workload was a quiet weather day across the continental United States. It is no wonder that most of the people that worked in the nerve center of dispatch and meteorology were either coffee drinkers or smokers and sometimes both.

The only cigarette I ever smoked was as a freshman in college during an impromptu autumn softball game. Several friends were hanging out by first base when one of them offered everyone a cigarette. How bad could one cigarette be? While I never took up the habit, my father was a smoker for a number of decades before he quit cold turkey when I was ten. The aroma of cigarette smoke never bothered me. Like a number of students, I accepted and was offered a light. Not inhaling my first puff, the one who offered me the cigarette looked over and said that it wasn't worth smoking if I didn't inhale. My second drag was big and intentional. I inhaled. What happened next I could never have anticipated. My lungs seized for a few seconds. That was followed by the deepest, uncontrollable coughing I had ever experienced and the feeling as though I would not be able to catch my breath. I thought I was going to die. That was my first cigarette, and it was also my last.

Coffee was another story. Coffee seemed as natural as a glass of water since coffee milk, a New England staple, was always available when I was growing up. One of the side effects of getting used to coffee milk was that it translated to my always needing cream and sugar for hot coffee in the morning. That's still generally true today. Only on rare occasion will I drink coffee black and with just cream and no sugar. With a cup of coffee in my hand most of the day, I fit right into the general flow of working at Northwest Airlines.

Several months had gone by and I was slowly getting better at managing the workload. I knew everyone in "metro" (pronounced with a long "e" and short for the meteorology department) but there were so many dispatchers and pilots that popped in and out of metro so often that getting to know their names well was nearly impossible. That was about to change.

111

One morning, I poured myself a cup of unique cherry-flavored coffee from my thermos and set it on the weather briefing table. At that same moment one of the dispatchers, Pete Schenck, was briskly walking by to return to his desk. Several feet after passing my cup, he stopped dead in his tracks and turned back.

"Wow. That smells really good. What is that?"

I told Pete that it was a unique cherry-flavored coffee and asked him if he'd like to try some. He did and was quite enamored with it. We engaged in a fun, light conversation about coffee and discovered that we both liked it beyond its ability to keep us mentally sharp at the office. The stuff tastes great.

The work flow never stops at an airline and both of us needed to get busy again, Pete at his desk where he supported dozens of flights simultaneously and me at the plotting table where all of our high-level charts were carefully analyzed. As I sat there plotting pilot reports from aircraft speeding across the Atlantic Ocean, I wondered if our paths were Divinely crafted to intersect. I always tell people to hold on tightly to the friends that God masterfully places in your life because those are the ones that will bring you the greatest joy. Even in those brief few minutes, I sensed that Pete was one of those special people that would journey with me for many miles ahead.

When my forecasting shift ended, I drove home with a new mission: Find another bag of that cherry coffee to bring to Pete. Fortunately, the gourmet grocery store at which I found the coffee in the first place still had some in stock and I gleefully went to the register with only that one item. I think I was as giddy as my college friend, Bob Brickey, when he was toting that delightful bottle of amaretto for me less than ten years prior.

I brought it in with me the next day and placed it on his desk. I could hardly wait to see the expression on his face. Not long after, I heard Pete's unmistakable laugh as he discovered the coffee. While our friendship may have started with the aroma of that unique coffee steaming from my mug a day earlier, it was eternally cemented a day later. After that, there wasn't a single day that went by that we did not share some time at each other's desk.

In no time, Sally and I had been delightfully adopted and grafted into their family in a special way. I realized this after being invited to their home for our second Thanksgiving in Minnesota. Both Sally and I were far away from our respective home towns and our work schedules would not permit a trip back east for the holiday. Pete and Mindy insisted we have Thanksgiving dinner with them.

While their home was beautifully decorated, and had a stunning view of one of the coves on Prior Lake and the warm scents of turkey and stuffing at every turn, there was something much more valuable that awaited us. It was the unmistakable awareness that Pete and Mindy, along with their two beautiful young daughters, had adopted and grafted us into their family. Never before outside our respective families had either of us ever felt such a genuine love as well as an eagerness to connect with us beyond simple friendship. For the first time since moving to Minnesota more than a year prior, it felt more like the place we were supposed to be. That went a long way to giving me peace. Instead of forever looking ahead to calculate the next career move, I was satisfied with where I was.

At the end of the evening, Mindy insisted on making me some turkey sandwiches for my shift at Northwest the next day. It came with all the fixings. Sally and I basked in the joy of the evening as we drove back to our home in Wayzata.

The coffee episode was the introduction. The Thanksgiving meal at their Prior Lake home was the time and place where a deep connection was made for keeps. It was the beginning of many special times together at their home, ours, and at adventurous restaurant outings.

One of several memorable restaurant visits was to "Windows On Minnesota," a stunning bistro on the 50th floor of the IDS Tower, Minneapolis' tallest building near Nicolette Mall (made famous by Mary Tyler Moore's iconic hat toss in her 1970s television sitcom). While the food fare was outstanding and the fellowship joyful, there were two things about that evening out that have been welded permanently into any remembrance of our dining experience. The first was that despite having a beautiful table near the window, we had no view. Every once in a while, the tallest building in Minnesota is the least desirable place from which to view the city. A low overcast shrouded the top half of the building and the cloud cover was so thick that the only thing we saw was the dim, orange glow of the high pressure sodium lamps on the roof. Out of the four people enjoying dinner around that table, two of them were meteorologists. Pete and Mindy took joy in ribbing Sally and me about picking "Windows On Minnesota" knowing better than anyone that the stunning Minneapolis skyline would be totally obscured from view. The second was when the bill came. Months earlier, I purchased an *Entertainment Book* and was surprised to see a coupon for the ritzy, "Windows On Minnesota." Before leaving the house, I located the coupon, tore it from the book and slipped it in my wallet. After the check came, I pulled out some cash and, without a second thought, the discount coupon was placed on top. You might have thought I placed a tarantula on the table. A coupon at what is arguably one of the finest dining locations in the state? It has been over twenty years since our first meal there and I still cannot shake the reputation of being a coupon clipper. Almost every time we go out to dinner now, Pete asks if I have any coupons.

After more than a year of cranking out upper level wind forecasts, selecting the tracks that our trans-Atlantic flights would fly and producing the host of surface products that supported the flight and ground crew, boredom had surfaced. It wasn't the work itself. That I found interesting and it would serve me well as a general aviation pilot down the line. The boredom crept in after coming to the conclusion that virtually all aspects of forecasting for an airline required very little creativity. I could not put my finger on my restlessness at first. That moment came one day while preparing the one product that I dreaded the most, the airport destination forecast. This was the short-term forecast used by pilots to inform their passengers what weather to expect at their destination.

At the time, we serviced hundreds of destinations nationally and internationally. Twice a day, we had to produce a surface forecast for each of the destinations. Not having the luxury of hours to look over all the data available like there is for a meteorologist working for a single television station in one city, we all had to do the best we could to come up with a forecast that would prepare the passengers for their arrivals. On top of that, the forecast had to be completed in one or two short words with a forecast maximum and minimum. With such a restriction, there simply isn't a lot of room for creativity.

Instead of remaining frustrated in my boredom especially in this task, the creative juices that God gave me began to bubble to the surface once more. Forget using the usual "sunny," "partly cloudy" or "rain" (we were not allowed to use the word, "thunder"). I began using some of the descriptives that I liked using in television. Soon, I began introducing forecasts such as, "milky sun," "drizzmal" and even one that piqued the interest of pilots and passengers, "NACITS," an acronym I coined in 1982 in Cedar Rapids, Iowa at KGAN-TV-2 which means "Not A Cloud In The Sky."

Within days, my attitude changed. While still a time bandit and lower priority item, generating the destination forecast was no longer a dreaded part of my day. Pilots and dispatchers alike went out of their way to tell me how much they and their passengers enjoyed the unorthodox, quirky and fun forecasts.

Weeks later, one of my coworkers quietly pulled me aside to let me know that smoke was beginning to rise from the office of the director of meteorology over my destination forecasts. What little creativity I brought to the table was about to be extinguished. Before I even had the chance to stew about it, he gave me the manager's direct quote: "André needs to understand that he is not doing weather on television while he is here."

It was that quote that set several things in motion. The first was that of being insulted for being part of an honorable profession prior to coming to Northwest Airline. It was as if he was saying that broadcast meteorology was not serious work and airline meteorology was. The second was anger for taking away the little creativity that was giving joy not only to me but to many pilots and dispatchers. The third thing was my realization that perhaps I was not well suited to making Northwest Airline a place from which I would retire. In hindsight, I now see it as God's nudge to get me back on track with what he had planned for me.

The manager kept his door open and unlocked even when he was not there. For reasons I cannot remember, I walked into his office and found a "things to do" note pad. One of the items was to talk to me about my destination forecast. I had all night to think about it. After settling my spirit, I wrote the manager a note informing him that I would return to using less descriptive forecasts and left it on his desk. One of the final tasks of that shift that day was to issue the destination forecast. I dreaded it once again.

The revelation I had was no less obvious than a baseball beaner. As I issued the dry, colorless destination forecast before heading out the door that day, I knew in my heart that I did not belong there. The Lord gave me the need to be creative and I could not exercise it in an airline meteorology office. Not only was broadcast meteorology an honorable profession but both the earning potential and the working hours were much better as well. My mind was resolutely convinced that it was time to go.

It was little consolation that, for weeks, both pilots and dispatchers began asking where all the "fun forecasts" were. The objections never came from the people it was meant to both help and entertain but stemmed from no more than one or two people inside our own department. My frustration disappeared very quickly and was replaced by a kind of sadness. How sad it was to know that there were people in the world who were missing out on the contagiousness of joy and creativity.

Pete's heart was heavy over the whole affair as well, making known his disappointment both to me and to the managers over seeing an abrupt end to the amusing forecasts. While Pete may not have known those specific things I resolved in my mind, he could sense that my heart was no longer in my work. It had become just another means to a paycheck. I could see it in his eyes every time we spoke. While it was completely unspoken, there was something in Pete's countenance that told me that he understood that I needed to plot a course in a different direction.

During my tenure at Northwest, I maintained a finger in the broadcasting pie by hanging out with the people at KARE-11. Because of my background, they readily made fill-in work available as opportunities came by. It was the best of both worlds. The travel perks at Northwest Airline could not be beat and with most of my family along the east coast, that was a plus. When my schedule allowed, I took joy in stepping in front of the camera to release some of the creativity that I was forced to leave outside the dispatch office at Northwest.

For months I quietly started sending out my resumé and video samples of my work at KARE. Occasionally, interested stations would call and take conversations to the next level. Only twice did the conversations lead to a serious offer. For reasons that came from deep within my gut, I declined both. The right opportunity had not yet come along.

The summer of 1987 was winding down. One day I was sitting in the KARE-11 weather office keeping Sally company during one of my off days when we started joking around about what it would be like to do a husband and wife weather segment. Out of that conversation, we had fun writing a pilot promotional spot for "Couples Weather Week." At the end of the promo, Sally and I begin arguing about the weather before the video faded to black. Telling a few others about our idea, the production crew wanted to shoot the promo for kicks. We had fun putting it together and had a few laughs watching it. (It's up on YouTube. Do a search for "KARE test promo.")

Somehow, unbeknownst to us, a copy of the videotape ended up on the news director's desk. A number of days later, both Sally and I were summoned to his office. After we sat down, Tom Kirby reached behind him and waved the video cassette that both of us recognized as being the mock promo. My mind was racing. How was I going to explain using station resources to have a little fun? Tom surprised us both.

"This is fun stuff! A week is too short, though. I think we ought to try this for a month. When can we start this?"

In light of the direction to which I had made a heart commitment, the door of opportunity seemed to fly wide open. It was a calculated risk for which I wasted no time.

"How about something easy like September first?"

"Fantastic. With the both of you doing segments together, it would make sense to put one of you outside in the elements and to have you banter in a split screen. The first thing we need to decide is who will be outside," Tom looked back and forth waving his finger.

KARE made outdoor weather trendy by designing a landscaped backyard that was attached to the news set via a stunning glass greenhouse whose on-air weather segments were popularized by chief meteorologist Paul Douglas.

All it took was a few seconds for Sally to cringe at the thought of standing outside at the break of sunrise on a winter morning in skirt and heels while backyard thermometers were well below zero and wind chills were approaching minus sixty.

"He'll do that," she was pointing to me before I even knew she had whipped out her finger. It was settled. I was going to be, "Mr. Outside," and Sally would be "Mrs. Inside."

We left Tom's office on that mid-August morning in a dreamlike daze. Later that morning, I typed my letter of resignation to Northwest Airlines, drove down to the dispatch center and walked into the my manager's office to personally deliver the letter. With all honesty, I did not know what kind of reaction to expect given some of our differences. The conversation could not have been any more cordial. He was not surprised and even half expected it. He also seemed to understand my need to channel that deeply ingrained creative drive in a place that thrives on it.

Pete was working that afternoon and I stopped by to quietly let him know what had just transpired. I could see a mix of emotions in his eyes. I relished the look of excitement and pride. Mixed in that look was an element of sadness from the thought of not having the luxury of immediate access to each other as before. Thankfully, as it turned out, our leisure time together actually became more frequent and meaningful after my last day at Northwest.

Despite the confidence with which I envisioned my professional U-turn back into the world of broadcasting, I wondered how everything would play out in the end. Tom Kirby and KARE-TV thought enough of the idea to try the tag team, husband-wife fusion for not one week but for the entire month of September. I had enough belief that this was the right place and right time for my U-turn that I left my secure position at the airline to take flight into this television experiment as a freelancer, without a contract and without any guarantees that it would extend beyond the last day of

September. I felt a little like Christopher Columbus who, in 1492, had set sail on a passionate hunch on which there were no guarantees. Five hundred years separated the journey that both he and I simply had to make.

KARE-11

For me, there was always a sense of magic and wonder when it came to broadcast facilities, both radio and television. They drew me like no other places could.

Some of my earliest memories from my elementary school days include the fascination of how NBC's "Today Show" could project the nation's weather map using some kind of rear projection onto a large screen. I would spend hours upon hours trying to recreate the same process in our darkened bedroom at night or by using the sun as my projector during the day. During the sixth grade, I joined the newly formed Explorer club whose focus was television. Our sponsor was WTEV-6's audio announcer, Ben Schnieder, who welcomed us into the world of television every other week. In the late summer of 1973, the brand new New Bedford High School opened its doors for my freshman year. After I discovered the state-of-the-art television studio in the heart of the campus, the studio's director and manager, Barry Mangan, could not get rid of me. I spent as much of my free time there as I could and eventually convinced Mr. Mangan that he needed to include weather in the school's monthly, pre-recorded student newscast which was beamed to all four lunchrooms and all three lunch periods on black and white monitors. And then there was radio. I would frequently bike my way to visit the two local New Bedford radio stations, WNBH and WBSM, the latter of which gave me my start in the real broadcast world.

Channel 11 in Minneapolis was no different. An adrenalin rush was always waiting for me when I stepped into its newsroom which was always buzzing with activity. Even the smell of electronics and very cool, conditioned air that awaited noses just inside the rear employee entrance jazzed me.

The powerhouse media company, Gannett (publisher of *USA Today*), purchased the station in 1983 at a time when one employee recalls that the early evening newscast was in fourth place behind reruns of "Leave It To Beaver." Having little to lose, the avant-garde news managers took a number of calculated risks and redefined local news and how it was done. By the time Sally was hired in the late summer of 1985, "KARE-11 News" had gone from dead last in the ratings to first place. The news team was having loads of fun and it was obvious to the growing audience.

In the same way that John Coleman plowed new ground on "Good Morning America" in 1976, Paul Douglas, KARE-11's chief meteorologist hit Minnesota's ground running. Instead of using the well-defined, traditional pathways of doing television weather, Paul blazed a new trail into unknown territory.

During his college years at Penn State, he drove to Scranton on weekends to do WNEP-TV's weather segments. WNEP was one of the first stations in the country to develop an outdoor weather segment. If you stop to think about it, outdoor weather makes perfect sense. It's where the weather is. Getting current conditions correct is never an issue when your studio ceiling is the sky.

Not long after Paul arrived at KARE in 1983, he made a tongue-in-cheek suggestion that they start doing the weather outside to which Tom Kirby answered, "Do you know how cold it gets here in the winter?" But the idea had enough appeal to move ahead. Months later, not only was a beautifully landscaped outdoor set designed but it was attached to the indoor news studio by a greenhouse enclosure to allow the talent to move from studio to outside and back as needed.

Paul's weather segments from the "KARE-11 Backyard" were the talk of Minnesota by the time we entered into the picture, but it wasn't always like that. According to Paul, the audience didn't know what to think of the segments. Because it was something that was so out-of-the-box, it took a year or two before much of the audience could decide if they would embrace the concept. Embrace it they did. Only Paul, with his youthful, homespun charm and wit, could have accomplished this result so quickly.

I suspect this was possible only because the audience sensed that his charm was genuine and humble. Paul and his wife welcomed us into his life and world and made us feel like Minnesota was home. More than that, he unknowingly modeled an important element of broadcast meteorology that I had not yet been able to grab a hold of. That element was having fun.

Up to this point in my career, I had seen the value of grabbing on to at least one dimension of the art of television that I could master easily and to build the rest of my slowly percolating abilities around it. That mastery came in creating what we in the business call eye-candy, that is, the knack of being able to create things that are visually interesting, colorful and aesthetic. I suspect it was something that naturally developed during my school years since I was always trying to place the right chart, graphic or photo on my assignments so that they had an optical appeal and thus a better chance for a higher grade. Once in college, the media began to include the television screen since my alma mater, Lyndon State College, had an on-campus television studio where meteorology students were able to deliver weather segments three times a day to the local cable audience. No longer limited by paper, the television screen offered many unique possibilities.

I can still remember preparing one of the graphics for an evening weather segment. My aim was to add some attractive, eye-popping animation to a forecast map. Before the advent of the all-powerful weather graphics computers, I had to manually draw each temperature on the United States map to which one of our cameras was pointed and run back to the editing bay and edit in a fraction of a second of the new frame. That process took me well over a half hour. The resulting animation took no more than two seconds to play. But that two-second animation caught the attention of the media department's director. After the newscast was over, he asked me the one question that made the effort worthwhile.

"How did you do that?"

That question only fueled me to dream up other ways to make our weathercasts visually stimulating and interesting.

When I moved to Cedar Rapids after graduating, I was fortunate enough to land at one of only a handful of television stations across the country to have a weather graphics computer. Remember, this was 1981 when the overwhelming majority of television stations in both large and small markets had the standard wall maps on which the meteorologist would use everything from gooey, water-based markers to bulky, magnetic numbers and symbols. We, too, had the wall maps but we also made use of a first generation computer that had 8-bit graphics that had to be programmed line-by-line. The more elaborate the computer graphic, the longer it took to program. (You can sample the forecast graphics by doing a YouTube search for "KGAN weather Andre Bernier." That weathercast was from December of 1981.)

The painstaking process did not discourage me from trying to jazz up the weather segments visually. Because my confidence level and delivery still needed a ton of work, having that one thing that I knew that I could master and rally around prevented me from succumbing to the kind of discouragement that eventually squeezes many good people out of the business. Without that Divine gift, I would very likely be doing something entirely different.

Only months later, I was at the launch of "The Weather Channel" learning how to operate some of the most sophisticated electronic graphics computers. They were so cutting edge, that John Coleman had secured a one-year exclusivity on what was known as the Quantel Paintbox. It was the first one sold in the United States. The serial number on that Paintbox was Number One. The artists hired were eager to take me under their wing and to encourage my creativity while showing me how to harness the power of the Paintbox.

While conjuring up ways to add the "eye-candy" to segments which I anchored, I was delighted to see that a few of my co-workers wanted to incorporate some of the material into their on-air segments. There were also others who thought I was trying to grandstand, dubbing my segments as, "André's laser show." It may have been an expression of distaste, but I saw it as a compliment.

That element of creativity was absent when I worked for the Minneapolis radio station. In order to keep my visually creative instrument sharp, I would often visit Sally at KARE-TV and start fashioning complex weather animations for her weather segments as well as Paul's. My motive was simple. I enjoyed creating them and took pleasure when the on-air staff would insist on using them. It wasn't long when the news director, Tom Kirby, made a mental note that I had become a part of the KARE-TV fabric because of the time I invested in creating slick weather graphics just because I enjoyed doing it.

Eventually, a scheduling conflict arose in the weather office and they needed a warm body to fill in for a weekday morning weather slot. Tom asked if I would be willing to pinch hit. With no other conflicts getting in the way, I told him that I would.

I tried getting a good night's sleep the night before, but sleep completely escaped me. I was far too excited and tossed and turned all night until finally getting up at three in the morning feeling like I had already consumed several cups of espresso. When the red tally lights starting glowing, there was sense of motivation and earthly purpose that I realized that I could get nowhere else. With a thumbs-up of approval from Tom during the daily morning meeting that followed, I knew that I would be getting more work whenever the opportunity arose.

One of the philosophies that became the overriding current on which KARE-TV operated was that of creativity. Everyone was forever encouraged to explore new territory.

"Don't ever be afraid to try something new on the air," Tom would remind us, "and do not concern yourself about whether you think I would like or dislike it. Don't worry. If I don't like it, I'll tell you and we'll move on. Go out there and have fun."

New things we did try, and KARE-TV had no problem with riding that philosophy to give a husband and wife team the go-ahead to anchor the weekday morning weather segments together.

Car pooling could not have been any more fun than it was for Sally and me beginning on that September morning. Waking up together, having breakfast together and riding into the station together was reason enough to know that I was going to enjoy this new adventure. In the pre-dawn dark, we noticed several boxes neatly leaning up against the back door. Our names were written on them and I recognized the handwriting immediately. Pete had preceded our arrival.

We opened the boxes in the light of the weather office and found a beautiful corsage for Sally and a sharp carnation for my suit jacket. The thought that Pete drove 45 minutes in the wee hours to make sure that we had these tokens of his and Mindy's affirmation made us grateful beyond words.

Everyone on staff that day, both on- and off-air, seemed to enjoy this quirky deviation. The segments went as well as we had hoped and the first review during the morning meeting that followed the newscast in Tom's office was equally encouraging. Tom liked what he saw. Nonetheless, Sally and I spent two weeks trying to find any groove that would give the weather tag team concept real legs on which to run. While we were having a blast, there seemed to be something missing in the chemistry.

We stumbled onto the catalyst we were looking for quite by accident one morning during our third week. On this particular day, I drove in before Sally and prepared all the graphics and forecast before she came in. During one of our on-air segments where we faced each other in a "split screen," I mentioned to Sally how it would have been nice to see a little sun, but that it would stay cloudy all day. To my surprise, she chimed in quickly.

"Oh, I think we will see some sun. Don't you?"

"Not at all. My money is on cloud cover all day."

"Wanna bet?"

Inside that short fifteen-second exchange, the studio became electric. On live television, a bet had been made between two meteorologists who had different opinions and happened to be husband and wife. The news anchors could easily see that, while the banter was playful, there was a delicate marital tension that had developed right before their eyes.

After that on-air exchange, we walked back to the weather office wondering if we could milk this for all it was worth. It was clear that the anchors were having a field day with it, so in the next weather segment, Sally and I went further by outlining with great specificity the rules of the wager. Dinner at a fancy restaurant was on the line. If it remained cloudy all day, I would win. If the sun came out and cast shadows where we were standing at any time during the day, Sally would win. The anchors and crew were placing bets of their own on each of us during the newscast.

After our local morning and network newscast ended, we walked into the news director's office for the morning meeting. Tom was smiling from ear-to-ear. It had taken a couple of weeks, but this was the husband-wife rivalry that he was hoping would make the weather-couple concept the talk of the town. And indeed it was. Tom was so pleased with what had transpired on the air that he insisted on paying for our dinner no matter who won.

I felt pretty smug when sky kept its dull, gray cast virtually all day. Sally and I were in our living room looking out the big picture window facing south when we both noticed one very small hole in the clouds. While Sally insists that the size of the hole keeps getting smaller every time I tell the story, I maintain that it was the size of a dime held at arm's length. I chuckled at its size. What is the chance that such a small hole in the clouds will allow enough of a ray of sun to cast shadows in our backyard?

Within minutes, it was clear that the ray of sun poking through the overcast might cast shadows a little too close for comfort. As Sally started smiling broadly, I shook my head in disbelief. The sun beamed down on our home. For about fifteen seconds, the time it took for the weather couple to make the on-air wager, our shadows were distinct. Worse yet, our neighbors on either side of us did not have enough sun to cast shadows!

Needless to say, Sally took gleeful satisfaction in retelling the story for our audience the next day and it provided wonderful fodder for follow-up newspaper stories and public appearances. Based on the mock promo we cut for "Weather Couple Week," it was exactly what Tom Kirby was hoping would emerge - The kind of fun husband and wife rivalry that made television couples like Ricky and Lucy Riccardo ("I Love Lucy") and Cliff and Claire Huxtable ("The Bill Cosby Show") resonate with the audience. It took a slight difference of opinion and a hole in the cloud deck to take the weather-couple concept from ordinary and forgettable to unique and memorable.

While there were other similar events that flavored the weekday morning weather segments from that moment on, none was talked about more by the audience than that first squabble. In hindsight, it was likely the element of surprise which both of us genuinely expressed which authenticated the impromptu exchange. Had the exchange been planned, it would not have looked so priceless.

It seemed like Sally and I had just started to find the sweet spot when September was drawing to a close. We wondered if we had convinced Tom to keep the weather couple in place. A quick meeting with him on the last day of September gave me reason to sigh with relief and gratitude.

"Let's keep going with this. I like what I see. It's fun stuff," he said with his camouflaged manager's smile.

It was time to relax and enjoy the treat of working side by side with Sally. Having the luxury of occasionally stopping at our favorite breakfast nook on our way home after work was a delightful indulgence. Nonetheless, even the most perfectly matched marriages need some healthy "alone" time. After all, we were now riding to work together, working together, riding home together and spending much of the rest of the day together. We both relished Saturday mornings for different reasons. Since the shift required smacking an obnoxious alarm hours before dawn broke every weekday morning, it was her chance to sleep in long enough to see the sunbeams gently wake her instead of the alarm clock. After experiencing body-jarring shift changes every three weeks at Northwest Airlines, I preferred keeping my sleep schedule as stable as possible. That, in and of itself, was a real treat. Often before sunrise, my solo time was a big breakfast at one of several breakfast eateries with the morning paper or a book that I was reading.

October and November became a honeymoon period for me at KARE-TV. While I was still a freelancer, it was a full-time position which appeared to be stable and secure. Those who for so long encouraged me to be patient and persistent were now celebrating my ingress into the Minneapolis television scene. Besides Paul Douglas, director Frank Stackowitz and film critic and long time weather personality Barry Zevan always went out of their way in order to make me feel like I was an important part of their professional world. As small as they think their gestures were, it was paramount in my slow but steady journey toward a time when any remaining performance insecurities would slowly disappear leaving only the joy and passion that propelled me into this profession when I was a youngster.

George The Mailman

As the air grew colder and the first ice started forming along the miles of Minnesota's lakeshores, I began to wonder where this experiment would eventually lead. As stable as my position was with KARE, it was still freelance. There was no indication that any long-term contract was being considered in the short run. While there were a few possible "rearrangements" in the weather staffing in the coming year, nothing was imminent. I began to wonder if I should be sending out some feelers outside the Minneapolis market.

December arrived. Everything was beginning to look very festive. Houses and business were brightly decorated with lights which looked even more festive now that the snow cover had given them a Thomas Kinkade glow. Even the KARE studios were becoming difficult to navigate as the piles of "Toys For Tots" donations grew daily, a tradition that gave the audience a sense of ownership as the very toys they brought in were placed in plain view of virtually every camera angle. My friend, Pete, coordinated the Northwest Airline employee contribution to the drive every year with voluminous deliveries every week or so.

The morning show had ended and the morning meeting was long finished when Sally and I were casually tidying the office before heading back to our home in nearby Wayzata. The phone rang and Sally answered it. I could tell by the way she started responding that it was someone we knew. It didn't take me long to conclude that Sally's mother had called. After a few minutes, Sally handed me the phone.

"Hey there! I was reading this morning's *Plain Dealer* and came across an article about Channel Eight that I thought you may want to know about," her voice clearly excited about something.

Sally's mother read the article to me over the phone. It was in the media section and it was an interview with Virgil Dominic, news director of the number one station in Cleveland, WJW-TV-8. He talked about the new morning newscast beginning after the first of the year and that all of the anchors were in place except for a meteorologist. They were still looking.

This was it.

Out of all the openings for which I had interviewed in the past several years, I just knew that this was the one that I had been waiting for. How else can you explain turning down an offer to finalize a deal with the managers of a midwest television station who were eager to jump into their corporate jet and fly to Minneapolis? Or the chance to move back to my native New England at a station that made me an offer without asking me to fly in for an interview? While so much of me wanted to jump at these opportunities, my Divinely-guided intuition said, "No."

After placing a call to longtime Cleveland weather icon, Dick Goddard, I prepared an express mail package with my videotape and resumé that he would deliver personally to the news director.

Arriving at the Wayzata, Minnesota post office less than a half mile from our home, I looked at the post office that had become so familiar in the last several years and had the stronger than usual suspicion that this was the last resumé tape I would ever hand over to George.

While the Wayzata post office had a host of government employees buzzing about its stately brick building only a few blocks from the shores of Lake Minnetonka, George was the only person whose face I can still clearly see in my mind. He was the ever-present smile that treated every customer as if their needs were the most important thing in the world.

George saw me every couple of weeks with a videotape and resumé in my hands. Sometimes it went express mail. Sometimes the package was sent as the slower and less expensive media mail.

No matter what services I selected, it was always held in high regard.

"O.K. Let's see. This one is going to Boston. Isn't that near your hometown?"

George was amazing with the amount of detail he absorbed. While processing the package for departure, he would always ask about previous tapes and resumés, even those mailed months before. His inquiries went beyond the usual happy-chat. His interest was genuine.

George lived in a nearby town and had two daughters and a lovely wife. He bragged about each of them and how blessed he was to be surrounded by such a great family. From our conversations, he knew just how hectic life could be on our schedule and in our profession, but expressed the desire to see if we could get our families together to share a meal at their home sometime. It was an appealing idea. The thought of doing so brought images of dropping by Aunt Bee and Sheriff Andy Taylor's home in Mayberry, something easy to imagine since there was quite a resemblance between George and Sheriff Taylor.

Sometimes I wondered why I bothered sending out so many tapes and resumés. It was a lot like fishing. Many times the line was quiet and the bobber just sat there motionless. From time to time, there was a nibble. Less often, a nibble would lead to a full-blown tug on the line, only to reel it in and find that it was a kind of fish that you did not want, tossing the fish back into the water. George must have seen the discouragement in my face from time to time.

"You know, André, one of these days, one of these packages will lead to something very worthwhile. I have mixed emotions about that because our family loves to watch you and Sally right here in Minnesota."

He was always quick to fill everyone's cup with motivation. It seemed to be his gift.

It was a cloudy and cold December day in Minneapolis. The air was crisp and the clouds were occasionally shaking loose a few flurries. Aside from a sprinkling of salt, the seven cement steps that I climbed to the post office's door were pristine, free of snow and ice. George was waiting for me as I placed yet another package on his scale. Perhaps it was the confidence with which I gave him this package or the overwhelming optimism I had as I told him that this tape was going to Cleveland. George smiled and said very little as he processed the express mail package. He could tell that this time, I had more than just a curious nibble on the line. He handed over my receipt and, as-was his custom, wished me luck. As I walked back out into a monochromatic scene, I wondered how long it would take to hear something. The waiting game began.

Dick received the package the next day and immediately ran it into the news director's office. I received a call from Virgil Dominic only forty-eight hours after learning about the opening from Sally's mother. He said that he liked what he saw and wondered if I would like to come for an interview and visit. After only a brief chat, we planned on my visit to Cleveland sooner rather than later.

I flew to Cleveland less than a week later, staying with Sally's parents instead of being put up in a hotel. Between meeting the staff and managers and engaging in several interviews, nearly four hours had flown by. I remember very little about the interview itself except for what turned out to be the last question posed by then general manager David Whitaker.

"André, what do you envision yourself doing in the long term, say, ten or twenty years from now?"

That was an easy one to answer. After moving thousands of miles away from home to my first television job in Iowa, moving another thousand or so miles to Georgia with all of my belongings stuffed in my 1981 Mustang, and moving back north another thousand miles to Minneapolis - all within four and a half year's time - I was growing weary of moving. The old adage for broadcast professionals was, and probably still is, "Have blow dryer, will travel."

In a very matter-of-fact, homespun way, I answered David's question with Virgil sitting right next to me.

"In my short television career so far, I have seen more of the country than many people see in their lifetime. All of that has been fun. But I think there comes a time in everyone's life when having to pack up and move everything gets old. I've hit that point. This will be my last move. I like Ohio. I like Cleveland. It's a great weather market. I'm looking forward to letting my roots go deep for a change."

I drew a deliberate breath and added one more thing, "If you hired me today, I can assure you that I will be here for a very long time. I can also tell you that if you hired me today and, for whatever reason, you fired me a month later, I would still remain in Cleveland and do something else for a living. Cleveland is going to be home."

They were unrehearsed words from my heart. After my answer, David and Virgil concurred that they had probed me enough. After breaking for lunch, they handed me a contract offer to look over and invited me to be a part of their new weekday morning newscast. I called Sally and told her the news. For Sally, who was born and raised in Cleveland, it was great news.

It was during the flight back to Minneapolis that I had the chance to reflect on everything that had transpired. It was nothing short of a series of Divinely-guided events that brought me to this pivotal life junction. From the moment I took the call from Sally's mother to the moment I was handed a contract offer was only eight days. Furthermore, the offer was given to me on the eighth day of December, a date significant for many reasons including that of my first date with Sally nine years previous. And it was Channel Eight.

What normally transpires in at least several months time took only eight days. Eight was a very good number.

Part of me hoped that KARE-TV thought enough of the weather-couple concept to make me a contract offer to stay, but my spirit sensed that it would not be the case. After meeting with Tom Kirby the next day, he was genuinely pleased to hear about my Cleveland offer. It was the same kind of pride one might see from a father to hear that his son landed a great job right after graduation. He was giving me his blessing.

I stopped in to see George at the post office the following week to give him the news that I would be leaving right after the holidays. There may have been a congratulatory smile on his face but I did sense a touch of sadness in his eyes. I told him that Sally would stay behind in the Twin Cities for a while longer. KARE-TV graciously agreed to release Sally from her contract as soon as our home sold so that she could join me in Cleveland. Because home sales in the winter typically slow down in Minnesota, we did not truly expect that to happen until spring at the earliest.

We hoped that despite the preparations for our move to Ohio, that our families could have dinner together at least once before we left. While I did fly to Minnesota every third weekend, Sally and I were so consumed with preparing the house for sale and the move to Ohio, that our dinner together never did take place.

There are some beautiful photos of the Wayzata post office on line these days. Even though we have not been in contact in over two decades, I can still see George's uplifting smile and forever-sunny disposition. Whether he realizes it or not, he was a minister that kept me in focus and energized every time I brought him one of dozens of videotape packages. Since the last videotape passed from my fingers to his, I'm sure that he has served tens of thousands of customers, each of whom he would treat with the same level of importance.

I don't know if George still works there. My guess is that he is retired or approaching retirement as I write this. It's also my guess that George would remember me and my packages well. That's just the way he operated.

A decade after leaving Minnesota, our son Noah was born. Because we watch little television at our home, Noah developed a love for books and the stories that came from them. As he grew into his toddler years, he would ask me if I could tell him a bedtime story when it was time to turn in. Enjoying the process of spinning an impromptu story line that would last long enough for his eyes to grow heavy as he giggled and smiled, I thought of George and began spinning tales about "George the mailman" and his adventures on his route in the fictitious town of Pilaf, Ohio. Perhaps Noah will carry George's adventures to his own toddlers someday. I predict that George's deliveries to Mrs. Sauerkraut and her mailbox that was forever falling off the house and to Pepe le Peu whose house he was always avoiding will re-emerge again in a few more decades. Who knows? Perhaps it will be their Grandpa who will spin the tales once more and honor the real George who encouraged my journey, one which covered life's shoreline along Minnesota's ten thousand lakes.

An Arctic Send-Off

The month of December by its very nature can coax almost anyone into its hustle and bustle. Our December, however, was even nuttier. In addition to the usual Christmas parties and dinners, we began preparing the house for the real estate market. We decided to re-paper the finished basement to bring it up to date and make it look brighter and more cheerful. After a long afternoon and evening of meticulously lining up each sheet, Sally moaned in obvious disgust and called me back into the basement an hour later. Virtually every sheet had peeled off. The old paper was like non-stick teflon. Removing the old paper was something we had hoped to avoid since the glue previous owners used was more like well-cured cement.

While house prep consumed a sizable portion of our December time budget, we did set aside time to enjoy the Christmas season. At the various holiday gatherings I savored the relationships I held special, knowing full well that I would soon be surrounded by hundreds of new people living along a lake that is over four hundred times the size of the lake on which I lived in Minnesota. Fortunately with Sally staying behind and attending to the house sale, saying goodbye was something I did not have to do since I planned to fly to Minnesota every month or so on weekends until the house sold, more likely in the spring or summer. Little did I know how much of my spirit I gave to my friends until the following summer when Sally and I pulled away from the shores of Lake Minnetonka for the last time as Minnesotans.

After a delightful New Year's long weekend, it was time to drive to Cleveland. An "Alberta Clipper" came by during 1988's first weekend freshening up the snowpack. As was often the case, the eye-watering, arctic winds lullabied Sally and me to sleep on Monday night. By early Tuesday morning, it was clear, windy, and brutally cold. The outdoor thermometer outside our kitchen window lacked its usual red column of alcohol. It had receded close to its bulbous home base at -17°F. After a big breakfast and a few cups of hot coffee, it was time to do battle with the arctic winds while driving southeast toward Ohio. Unplugging the GMC Jimmy's block heater from the garage extension cord, I wondered if I would ever have the need to use it again in Ohio. The Jimmy grudgingly turned over and within minutes I was waving "so long" one more time to Sally in the front window as I backed out and started driving into the deceptively inviting, deep dawn colors of a clear sky sunrise. The voluminous plumes of condensation from every tailpipe gave away the deception.

Long drives usually have a way of helping me process what is ahead if there is an significant life junction involved. It was so moving to Iowa. Fortunately, Sally was with me for that one. It certainly was so during my two-day drive to Georgia. And my two-day drive from my hometown of New Bedford to Minneapolis was also no different. I was looking forward to processing the excitement and anxiety I was now feeling over the next fifteen hours between Minnesota and Ohio.

As the sun came up over the horizon, it unveiled yet another artifact of the pure arctic air. Suspended in the air and swirling slowly about, ice crystals by the millions, better known as diamond dust, sparkled like miniature flash bulbs. I expected them to disappear with time, but they surrounded me for hours through Wisconsin and even northern Illinois. I reached Chicago a little after noon and saw that the temperature was not much warmer in the Windy City than it was when I left Minneapolis. Bank thermometers flashed -10°F. Tailpipes were still spewing out columns of condensation and the sun did very little to help warm the inside of the cabin. Then I noticed something I had never seen in my lifetime. The ice crystals were so ubiquitous and the arctic sunshine so bright that two halos surrounded me with a brilliant sky show. The first halo was the more common twenty-two degree circle around the sun. The second halo surrounded the entire sky in every direction, like a giant circle of light on top of you. It was connected to the smaller halo on each side and disappeared inside the smaller one around the sun. I later found out that this very rare phenomenon is called a prismatic parahelion and occurs mostly in the high arctic regions of the globe. Seeing it as a special blessing, I couldn't help smiling.

Chapter 7

The Longest Mile

On January 12, 2010, I set a new record that was initially established between May 22, 1959 and May 18, 1981. For eight thousand and thirty two days, I was content to have been a member of my father's and mother's home, and resident of New Bedford, Massachusetts. Not until I started writing this chapter did I realize that I have now exceeded that period, plus a couple hundred days. That makes this chapter of my life's journey the longest stretch.

That also means that this chapter will be the most difficult to write. In addition to walking a portion of the journey whose conclusion is still many decades away, there is also the lack of time. Like a fine wine, time has a way of adding character, depth and flavor to the journey. Time has the ability to frame events in the proper perspective. The closer I get to my current position on the timeline, the less perspective I have. It will be a little like comparing a beautifully-aged, dependable Cabernet Sauvignon, with this year's precarious release of Beaujolais Nouveau. As you start walking away from the Cabernet Sauvignon with me, I'll do my very best to have you sample the Beaujolais Nouveau that, in my best judgment, will go the distance.

Virgil Dominic

Like so much of my professional career up to now, I was once again standing at the gateway of unexplored territory, with a team of others hired to enter, explore and take possession of it. In Atlanta, it was the nation's first all-weather cable outlet. In Minneapolis, it was a never-tried, husband-wife tag-team weather segment. Now in Cleveland, it was the first local weekday morning newscast. I knew it would work. A Cleveland audience appetite had been growing for a bona fide morning newscast for years. Some markets, like Minneapolis, had successfully started them. People, by and large, were starting to rise earlier and earlier for a number of reasons. Access to news up to that point was something that commuters listened to on the radio while making breakfast, or driving to work.

The timing was perfect. We were in the throes of an old-fashioned winter pattern. Snowstorms would end up being the best promotional aid that we had heading toward the mid-February premier of *Newscenter 8 This Morning*. In fact, the weather was so abrasive the week before the debut, that management gave us the go-ahead to do live weather cut-ins during the CBS network morning news. It served as a fantastic promotion for the hour-long morning newscast which was saturated with weather segments.

The tempestuous winter kept my end of the newscast secure in the first few months. That was good. The ominous clouds rising from the talent union, on the other hand, were very unsettling. Up to this point in my career, I was never part of a trade union shop. Even at top-rated KARE-TV, the talent was so well taken care of that a trade union was never even a distant thought. When I accepted the offer to come to Cleveland, joining AFTRA (American Federation of Television and Radio Artists) was mandatory to be employed as talent. Weeks after arriving, the negotiations for a new labor agreement were not going well, and there were serious discussions about a talent strike. As well as the new morning newscast was being received by the print media and television audience, I couldn't help second-guessing my decision to come here. While I would have loved to have the assurance from KARE-TV that I could come back if the situation warranted, I knew that I would have to weather this new chapter in my journey. Anytime anxious moments came knocking on my door, Virgil Dominic was there to offer me a solid sense of peace, stability and unconditional acceptance. It would be just fine. In the end, it was.

Before coming to WJW-TV, I was very familiar with who Virgil was. In the 1960s, Virgil Dominic's voice boomed across America each afternoon on NBC radio news from their Cleveland bureau. Once he became news director at WJW, he began to build a news operation which was founded on mutual respect and loyalty. Everyone who I knew in the broadcast industry told me that getting a job offer from Virgil Dominic was an offer of stability. As my first year spilled over to my second and beyond, it was clear that job security and stability were benefits of his fundamental model of team-building. At no other station have I ever experienced the sense of family like I have at WJW. That was by design. Virgil was a protective father figure for his television family, and it helped us to weather some very interesting times in the years ahead of us.

Sally joined the team at WJW after Mark Koontz, our then second-in-command meteorologist, broke his ankle. We found out about his misfortune after I flew north to Minneapolis one last time to give Sally company on her drive home to Ohio. During her last morning on-air at KARE, I joined her on set just like we used to do. Our best friends, Pete and Mindy came with their two daughters to watch. Once the newscast wrapped up, we gave all of our friends, especially Pete and Mindy, long and tearful hugs before heading east into the hot, mid-morning sun. With cell phones not yet on the scene, we placed a call to Sally's parents from a public phone at a rest stop somewhere near Chicago. It was there that Sally's mother advised me that the station needed me back as quickly as possible. Mark was unable to drive due to a severe ankle accident.

I called Virgil immediately and told him that I was driving back to Ohio with Sally for good, and that she would gladly dive into the mix to help patch the holes in the on-air schedule. Sally was in the right place at the right time, and immediately began plugging into a few of the weather segments, while Mark began his months-long healing process.

One day, she was filling in on the noon newscast since I was filling in at night. Not long after starting a pot of coffee, I received a call from the assistant news director. Sally had become suddenly ill to the point where others insisted on taking her to the hospital. I was asked if I could come in to cover the noon weather segment, to which I agreed. Thirty minutes later, I parked the car in the station parking lot and walked into the back security entrance. Virgil was waiting for me in the hallway. His genuine concern for Sally was beyond obvious as we convened in the middle of the hallway.

"What are you doing here, André?" he inquired.

I had the sense that when Sally was taken to the hospital, he initially did not know I was called in to cover the shift, and that he was none too happy about what I was asked to do.

"I'm here to cover the noon wea....."

Virgil's voice interrupted mine with a reassuring smile, "Oh, no you don't. Your wife needs you by her side. Don't you worry about the noon weather segment. We can do without a weather segment if need be. You need to be with Sally right now, so you get going. Call me if you need anything..... *anything.*"

As I walked back to my car, I was warmed to the core by the thought that one of the most powerful men in broadcast media was far more concerned about the people under his care, compared to the product for which he was responsible. I knew I was working in a special place, not because it was far-and-above the number one television news operation in Cleveland, but because I was working with Virgil Dominic.

When I moved to Cleveland from Minneapolis at age twenty-eight, even though I had been on national cable television, and active in Minneapolis, a large market, it still felt like I was a small fish that went from a comfortable pond to an intimidating ocean. For a short time near the year of my arrival, Cleveland was in the top ten of America's television markets. I had to prove myself all over again in a new place, and earn the respect of new co-workers, most of whom were well-seasoned and long-tenured in northeast Ohio. There were days where I drove home wondering if I belonged here.

The encouragement I received from all of my co-workers in various ways gave me the energy I needed to keep swimming and growing. Two of my co-workers were especially helpful in the first couple of years at WJW. Perhaps it was because they recognized symptoms of the small-fish syndrome I was experiencing. Perhaps it was because they were in my shoes once, and wanted to gently embrace me into the high-speed lane of big-market television. Whatever the motivation, it was key to my sensing assimilation into the team.

Neil Zurcher, famous for his "One Tank Trip" segments, always took time to sit down with me in the weather office to let me know how much he enjoyed watching my weather segments. I knew he was sincere with the specific references to some of the new concepts I was trying to employ. His ten-minute chats invigorated me to stay the course even when I made several serious perusals into a radical career shift. So many of these visits seemed to be Divinely timed at critical points in my Cleveland journey.

Initially, my opportunities to fill in for long time weather icon Dick Goddard were few. But after a couple of years, I would occasionally find myself filling in for a few weekday evening shifts, alongside the very popular news anchor team of Tim Taylor and

Robin Swoboda. Both tried their best to make me feel at home, but it was prime-time sports anchor Casey Coleman who must have sensed I needed extra encouragement. While pacing in the green room waiting for my weather segment to come up, Casey would frequently find his way into the green room just to chat and get to know me. This simple act of kindness did more than he could have imagined.

My acceptance as one of the team players was complete when I watched Casey's sportscast from home one winter evening not long after WJW's annual televised Thanksgiving Day Parade from downtown Cleveland.   I was providing man-on-the-street segments, with occasional interviews with some of the parade units. During Casey's closing segment, Casey gave honor to me for withstanding the pain of having a parade car tire roll over and stop on my toes while I was interviewing news anchors Tim Taylor and Robin Swoboda, without that wringing as much as a whimper from me. Tim Taylor later asked me why I had a funny look on my face. It was because I had more than a thousand pounds of pressure crushing my toes! The relief when the tire rolled off my foot was heavenly. I thought I was home free until several of my toes began to throb at the end of the broadcast. By the time the sun had set, I could not even place a light sheet over my foot. I had a broken toe.

Instead of a slow motion replay of a great football catch or basketball dunk, Casey showed a slow motion replay of the moment the tire rolled over and stopped on my foot.

"Kudos to our friend André who proved to us that he can take a lickin' and keep on tickin'!"

It was a delightful surprise. To our viewers, it was a friendly ribbing. To me, it was a warm welcome into their professional inner circle. What was once regret for stepping too close to a moving parade car suddenly became an amusing memory. While Casey was not literally running alongside me when the parade car used my foot as a stopping block, he did figuratively go the distance to send me a message. He saw me as a fish that was welcome to swim in their school. No longer did I feel like a tiny goldfish in a huge lake.

Roger Mercier

It was the Saturday after Thanksgiving. Those called to host and anchor the live Thanksgiving Parade had been asked to arrive at 7:30 A.M. Cold, gusty daggers of wind blasted around every downtown Cleveland intersection. Pale shades of faint, blue-grey light gave the empty city streets an apocalyptic look. Fortunately Ron Gomez, the head of security at WJW, drove four of us from the station to the parade site in a van, and dropped us off near the reviewing stand and weatherproofed anchor booth. The engineers were scattered about, running cables from here to there, and checking connections. Despite their presence, the streets were still largely empty. The crowds would come soon.

Cold air has an odd way of accelerating someone's need to race to the restroom. I suspect it may have had something to do with all the coffee we drank. Now we had a major challenge. No merchants within ten blocks were open yet, and the nearest fast food restaurant was at least a quarter mile away.

Someone in our group noticed that the first set of double doors going into a downtown department store was unlocked. While the store itself was closed, at least we could hide from the brutally cold wind for a few minutes. Once inside, smiles broke out in the cozy vestibule. The wind was making a noisy fuss, occasionally trying to pull the glass doors open, but at least now it was powerless to drive us closer to becoming human popsicles.

We were all a bit startled when the inside door moved. When it opened, a jovial security guard greeted us as if he had been waiting for us to arrive. In a sense, he had been.

"Greetings, my friends. I know that you are all here for the parade, so if any of you need to use the restroom, just let me know. You can use the facilities on the first floor."

That news was heaven to our ears. He continued speaking, now directing his conversation directly to me.

"André Bernier," the guard articulated in a perfect French Canadian accent, "I know that you are from New Bedford. It's nice to actually run into someone else from New Bedford here!"

"You're from New Bedford?"

"I spent many a decade there running around Acushnet Avenue and Saint Anthony's Church in my younger days. My name is Roger. Roger Mercier."

That made sense. Only a person of French-Canadian descent could have possibly pronounced my name in an accent I had not heard in decades. An instant bond formed. As the others drifted in and out of the first-floor door to take care of business, Roger and I monopolized the conversation. I asked him if he remembered my father's diner, The Diner Deluxe on Logan Street, next to the old Wamsutta Mill. He remembered the diner on Logan Street, but he was not sure if he had ever met my father.

After exchanging phone numbers, our group was being summoned to a mandatory pre-production meeting to prepare for the live, two-hour broadcast during which my foot would eventually be run over by one of the parade cars. Long after my toe healed, Roger remained true to his word. I began receiving regular phone calls from Roger encouraging me along the sometimes difficult road of broadcast news.

Roger's life journey ran deep with many detours, one of which gave him a special fondness for WJW. It was one of our engineers, Dick Lorius, who intervened in Roger's dangerous path. That intervention led Roger from alcoholism to decades of sobriety by the time we became friends. Roger was so grateful for Dick and others who cared enough to do something, that he spoke liberally about his rescue almost every time we spoke. He also affirmed that, without God's strength, his transformation to sobriety would not have been possible.

Talk is cheap unless it is backed up with some kind of tangible evidence. Discreetly, but with fervor, Roger was committed to attending regular AA meetings to provide support and encouragement to others. He was the recipient of that gift, and was compelled to pass it on as often as possible. The supernatural love that he possessed for each human being who came through the AA doors several evenings a week was unmistakable.

Roger had a notable sensitivity to those in the broadcasting industry. Perhaps it was due to his initial connection to someone in television who journeyed with him during his recovery that made him aware of the number of others from the industry who needed the same inspiration. He had a mission. In addition to the dedication he had to those trying to beat alcoholism, Roger also infused encouragement to those who shared his faith. That is why our friendship was so special.

In May of 2008, Roger was hospitalized. It was clear that his physical strength was waning. Through a mutual friend, Roger summoned me and news anchor Bill Martin to his bedside. In between newscasts, Bill and I drove over to his hospital room. He was in wonderful spirits and feeling much improved compared to several days before, yet Roger spoke to us as if he knew that his remaining time was short. Roger pointed out the window, then made a sweeping motion with his hand making reference to the people caring for him.

"There are so many people that need hope," he declared.

"Out there on the streets, even right here in this hospital and on this floor. I know. I've offered to pray for some of my caregivers, and they never refused. Don't forget about them. They need what you have. Listen, you have great visibility because of what you do.

Use the prestige that God gave you to give them hope. Trust me. They will listen."

After passing the proverbial baton, peace washed over Roger's face. His work on Earth was done. Bill and I anointed his forehead with frankincense oil, prayed over him, and left his room. On the way out, we passed by the same hospital workers that we saw on the way in, but somehow they all looked different. They were supposed to.

I enjoyed a few days off from work and, when I returned, a voice mail from Roger was waiting for me. He thanked me for coming with Bill. He sounded upbeat. Recovery was in his voice. A few more viewer voice mails later, a surreal message made me motionless at my desk. Roger was gone. He passed away peacefully only a few hours before I retrieved the messages. After doing so well, he had taken a dramatic turn for the worse in only a few hours. I had to go back and listen to Roger's message a few more times just to hear a voice that I would now have to wait until eternity to hear again. As much as I wanted to sit at my desk and reflect for a while, there was work to do. I had to make an attempt to focus on examining the skies beyond which Roger's spirit took flight.

While the honor was mine to pay my last respects at Roger's wake a few days later, many of his children and grandchildren raced over to spend some time with me. It wasn't because I was on television. They wanted to tell me how much Roger spoke to them about me. I didn't think I could miss Roger any more than I did, until they shared the high value he placed on our friendship.

I have the baton now, Roger. Thanks for helping me keep my feet on the ground and pointed in the right direction.

Dr. Kevin O'Connor

It was no surprise that it took a full year and then some for the chaos of moving to a new market to dissipate. The waves of uneasiness and second-guessing were remarkably similar to my move from Cedar Rapids to Atlanta. I spent most of my energy, and a better part of the first year, fending that off. By the second year, I was in a good groove. The morning show had quickly developed a solid audience that consistently placed us at number one in the ratings. It was time to coast for a while.

While spiritual growth was always something in which I had a casual interest in my pre-teen and teen years, it began to stagnate after leaving Atlanta. By the time we moved to Cleveland, it was a back-burner item. That changed two summers later. Life has an uncanny way of taking you to places that will oblige you to either reach beyond yourself by faith, or to convince yourself that no one can help you except yourself. The latter is a road full of anguish and torment. I am dumbfounded by the people who unnecessarily choose this lonely road.

In both Atlanta and Minneapolis, finding a church home was low on the priority list, dictated primarily by our wacky work schedules. Now for the first time since entering the broadcast world, my schedule had become much more stable. I had weekends off. That allowed me to begin the search for a church family.

Driving through Chesterland, it was difficult to ignore the appeal of the cute little white-steepled church near the corner of the main intersection. Even before setting my mind to finding a suitable place to worship, Chesterland Baptist Church had been the kind of church that made me smile as I drove by. I immediately placed CBC at the top of my short list of places to visit.

On a bright Sunday morning, I drove into the CBC parking lot and entered the back door where everyone else seemed to enter. I was immediately greeted by a joyful gentleman sporting a military-style crew cut, looking like a happy-go-lucky army sergeant.

"Hi, my name is André and I've never been here before. I'm wondering if someone can show me where everything is happening."

His eyes lit up, and he immediately introduced himself as Jack Puterbaugh, then called his delightful wife Eloise to be my personal escort. The pastor, Dr. Kevin O'Connor, a tall and stately man, commanded attention during the service with his noble Australian accent. More importantly, I felt welcomed as a friend and not as a local celebrity. It didn't matter who walked in the door. If someone new came to worship, they would have received the same warm welcome. It's no wonder why I often smiled just passing CBC.

I returned home from my first reconnaissance mission. Without reservation, I boldly announced to Sally that CBC was going to be our church home. Sally reminded me that I had agreed to visit all of the local churches before making a decision. Indeed, I did. For the following month or two, I visited virtually all of the local churches within five miles of our home. Each had its own charm, and each proved to be a worthy place to grow, but each Sunday I returned with the same conclusion. CBC was where God was calling us to be in this season of our lives.

As we became better acquainted with Dr. O'Connor, we quickly realized that he enjoyed adding humor in the things he did. He had a contagious laugh that actually sounded as if it had an Australian accent. During one of his Sunday morning messages, he admitted that one of his lighthearted ribbings led to quite a humbling experience. Prior to serving several churches in the United States, Dr. O'Connor and his wife Mary spent a number of decades as missionaries living with the people of Ethiopia. When he was able to break away from his work, it was common for he and his family to travel to Addis Ababa for a day at their busy marketplace. As he walked he passed a beggar who had one slice of bread in his hand, asking passers-by for money. Dr. O'Connor turned around and teased him, saying that he was hungry. The beggar motioned for him to sit down next to him. Dr. O'Connor did as the beggar asked. He was not prepared for what happened next. For the beggar that slice of bread represented life, and it was the only food he would likely see all day. He broke the bread in half and handed one of the pieces to Dr. O'Connor. It was one of the few times that I saw him weep with deep emotion from the pulpit, and there were very few dry eyes in the congregation. It was a native Ethiopian beggar who humbled a longtime pastor with a demonstration of generosity on a supernatural plane. Little did that beggar know that, fifty years later, someone halfway around the world would someday write about his act of extreme unselfishness. I am convinced that he is enjoying his just reward beyond this world.

Over time, Dr. O'Connor encouraged me to enroll in a distance education seminary. He administered a number of my proxy exams, and celebrated with me when each course's final grade returned. The courses took up all of my free time, yet when he casually mentioned that the church would be looking for a youth pastor to lead CBC's youth on Sunday mornings, I told him that I might be interested, but that I would need much more information about what was expected. Several weeks later, he announced from the pulpit that they had found their youth pastor. In a way, I was relieved to hear it since I already had my hands full with full-time work, and a full course load in the seminary extension program. Then he announced that the new youth pastor was in the congregation. My head started whipping around along with everyone else. Where was he?

His finger began to point, "And he is sitting right there."

My head was still scanning around when I suddenly realized that everyone else's head had spun around to look at *me*. I looked up to Dr. O'Connor. His finger had singled me out, and his broad Australian smile was all I needed to know that he would not accept a refusal. It was a tall order to fill, but I never had to fill that order alone. His door was always open, and I sat across from him many times for help.

Eventually, his wife Mary's health required that they move to a warmer climate. After much prayer and reflection, it was time for him to retire. I could not imagine CBC without him, even though CBC was founded in 1819 and has enjoyed a long history of wonderful pastors. Even in his well-deserved retirement near Pensacola, he continued to mentor me in ways I cannot count.

Bob Devine

Having been on the weekday morning show shift for more than two decades forces your body into a predictable rhythm. Even while enjoying time off, I often awoke before sunrise. Most of the time, my body woke me at just after five in the morning on days that did not require me to head to work. The house was always peaceful, and Sally was still fast asleep.

The routine, like a comfortable slipper, changed little. Grind some fresh coffee and start the brewer. Position my favorite chair by the sliding glass door with a cup of coffee on one side, and the Bible on my lap. It was the closest I came to enjoying a slice of heavenly peace here on earth. I had the sense that I had an exclusive audience with God, and I did.

If it was a weekday morning, my routine included turning on the radio just before six to listen to the start of a delightfully popular morning radio program called *Clock Watcher* on 103.3 FM, WCRF. The steadfast opening song, Leroy Anderson's *The Syncopated Clock*, performed by Arthur Fiedler, matched radio host Bob Devine's joyful greeting. While I had no idea what Bob looked like, I could picture him in my mind's eye as forever smiling.

In addition to the Godly perspective he brought to every aspect of the program, Bob had a keen sense of weather. His weather briefings went far and above reading the forecast from the

National Weather Service. There were interesting statistics important to the northern Ohio farmers and agriculturalists, along with detailed descriptions of weather systems all around the region. Weather was not just a necessary element of his morning radio broadcast. You could tell that he had a genuine fascination with it.

From time to time, I entertained calling WCRF to offer radio forecasting services, but almost as quickly as the thought came, I waved it off as being unnecessary since Bob did such an outstanding job of painting the day's weather outlook. The thought never had any traction until Jack Puterbaugh, one of the first people I ever met at the church we attended, suggested that I call WCRF to offer my services as their radio go-to guy for weather. Jack's prompt was all it took to give that idea new traction. After placing an initial call to general manager Dick Lee, he invited me to their studios to explore all of the options. I was also hoping to meet the man behind the familiar voice of the *Clock Watcher* morning program.

Shortly after speaking by phone, Dick and I met for a leisurely and comfortable talk about my offer to help in an unique way. When I was given the gift of a passion for meteorology at such an early age, I thought it would make a pleasant professional means by which to someday support a family. End of story. My spiritual journey and professional journey had a wide gap between them, and that seemed normal by all accounts. Except for sharing their origin, both seemed compartmentalized, separate from each other. Suddenly, I had the rare opportunity to give someone a tithe of my talent - literally. Because WCRF is a non-profit, non-commercial station, I offered to donate my time and talent to provide custom forecasts for their sizable and loyal audience. Dick had already spoken to Bob Devine about that possibility, and his response was one of warm welcome.

During the meeting, Dick asked Bob to join us so that we could meet. It is not uncommon to try to visualize what a radio personality looks like, but in the case of Bob Devine, I drew a blank, except for the timeless, broad smile with which I pictured him. Bob's tall and slender frame entered Dick's office, wearing that enduring smile that I had pictured through his radio voice. I was immediately comfortable.

Something else happened during that brief meeting that, up to that point, had never happened before in my lifetime. It took me by complete surprise. It is difficult to describe or to translate into words. The best way is to say that Bob beamed like a concentrated collective of hundreds of galaxies. Even though I had never experienced this kind of ethereal awareness, I immediately recognized it. What I saw is what happens when the Christ of the Bible, the Rescuer of the world, so fully indwells a human follower, that He adds an unspeakable brilliance to that person. That brilliance is not to be confused with the secular allure of a charismatic celebrity. Bob's luminous spirit was simply a reflection of someone greater than himself, identified by his authentic humility. Bob welcomed me and shared a genuine eagerness to partner together during his morning program. Even though his weather coverage was the best on Cleveland morning radio, he was more than willing to allow another voice to provide daily weather feeds.

Right from the get-go, Bob started a tradition that, even now long past his retirement, I still value. No matter how busy we were as we both approached the beginning of our broadcasts at just before six in the morning, Bob would always ask me, "How can I pray for you today?" Sometimes my request took on the form of a confession and shortfall. Sometimes it was something with which I was wrestling. There were also times of sharing joy and praise. Bob was never judgmental, and always encouraging, sometimes with a specific Scripture reference that he knew would be helpful. Remaining transparent was easy because my morning prayer partner was trustworthy.

After struggling himself with when to retire, in 2002 he believed that the time was right. His last broadcast is something I have in my CD collection. Not hearing his familiar voice during the mornings on which I enjoyed a day off proved to be something to which I never grew accustomed, even though one of my dearest friends, Mark Zimmerman, succeeded Bob in his weekday morning post.

Bob's final words at the end of his last morning program on September 29, 2002, was yet another example of how to run "Life's race" with exuberance, commitment and focus:

Well, what can I say? This is it. My service to you on *Clock Watcher* has come to an end. Do you think a farewell speech is appropriate? I think so. Here it is:

To sum up these years with Moody Bible Institute and WCRF, I would have to say that I have felt a lot like the Bible character Jacob in Genesis 29. You know the story, don't you? Remember how he wanted to marry Rachel, but his father-in-law-to-be gave him his daughter Leah instead. Recall how Jacob had to work seven more years just to get Rachel? But he said, 'These seven years have seemed like only a few days because of my love for her.'

Honestly, that's how I have felt about my service at WCRF. Almost. Because of my love for the Lord Jesus Christ and WCRF these forty-one years have seemed like, well maybe not like a few days, but would you believe a few months? I guess that's the way it is when you love what you're doing, and for Whom you are doing it.

Now, may I share an observation about you?

For a long time I have been convinced that you are among the most gracious, responsive and loving listeners in all the world. Honest, I mean that. Thank you.

As you know, I have used a lot of Scripture on *Clock Watcher* over the years. My prayer for you this Friday morning is that you'll be able to put into practice the Word of God that I've been able to share with you and then to teach it to your children.

Here's what I want so much for you... husband... wife... please spend time together in the Word of God and in prayer every day. I ask no more and no less. I can ask nothing better, right?

May God bless you mightily as you bear much fruit for the Lord Jesus Christ.

Bob Devine for wife, Wanda, until we meet again.

It has been nearly a decade since Bob offered that memorable farewell. Our paths have crossed on a number of occasions since then, and our emails and phone calls continue to be a source of encouragement. While Bob may no longer have twenty-five thousand watts available to propel his reassuring voice through the dawn, he still shines like a hundred galaxies whether he is speaking to hundreds from a pulpit or to a new friend at his backyard picnic table. It's that kind of light that made the path before my feet much easier to navigate.

Lawrence & Theresa Boone

In 1995, I was invited to come and deliver the Easter morning message at The City Mission in downtown Cleveland. In preparation, I designed a mock airline ticket to heaven as a part of the message's conclusion, but I needed several hundred copies. It was late Saturday afternoon, and I was running out of time. I stopped in at a local office supply store that I frequented to use their copier, but was informed that the copier was out of order. The only other option was their competitor a few blocks away.

I was relieved to see that their copiers were all operating just fine. I made my copies, but each sheet needed to be manually cut on their cutting board. It was a tedious task, but it had to be done.

Immediately to my right was an African-American woman just as busy as I was at another tedious task. I peeked over and saw that it was church-related, and I began a dialogue with her.

"I see we are trying to accomplish the same kind of thing," referring to the church-related material she was working on.

She introduced herself as Theresa, and she showed me what she was working on, and I gave her one of my "tickets to heaven," telling her that I would use it in my Easter message at the City Mission the next day. She then pointed to her husband, who was waiting for her in the car and who was the senior pastor of the downtown church. Before I left, she gave me one of their church bulletins and invited me to come and worship with them sometime.

"We don't care if you're white, black, blue, green, or from the moon. God loves everyone, so we would love to welcome you anytime."

Not once did I ever get the impression that she knew who I was, and that made her invitation even more endearing. In fact, our entire exchange was a pleasant treat. Just two soldiers of Christ working to the same end.

On the way out, I stopped at the driver's side window of the man she had said was her husband. He was deep in thought, reading his very well-worn Bible until I gently knocked on his window. Surprised that someone was standing there, he rolled down the window. I introduced myself, then he spoke up.

"Yes, I know who you are! To what do I owe this pleasure?"

I told him that if his wife seemed to be taking a bit more time than normal, it was because we had starting talking about our ministry printing projects. I wished him a happy Easter, and went on my way. Once in the car, I showed Sally the bulletin from Covenant Community Church, shared the story of meeting Theresa, and told her to hang on to the bulletin.

Before sunrise on Easter, Sally and I drove down to the City Mission. The space on campus used for the Easter service was packed, and the tickets to heaven that I used as a teaching tool were a big hit. A number of men told me that the ticket helped them to understand their part in receiving God's gift of eternal life.

When the service was over, the sun had brilliantly risen. It was still quite early. I had an idea. Instead of driving all the way back to Geauga County for our home church's Easter service, I suggested to Sally that we grab a quick bite to eat somewhere locally, and drive over to Covenant Community Church for Easter worship. After all, Theresa Boone did invite us.

We arrived at their Kinsman Road campus and boldly walked in to their sanctuary looking for the Boones. We were immediately warmly welcomed. The younger children and teens began to scramble, not because we were the only white faces inside their walls, but because "famous TV people" had just walked in, and they wanted to be the first to tell the Boones that we were looking for them. Hearing the news, but not believing it, Theresa walked up the stairs from the classrooms below to see for herself. Her jaw hit the floor when she saw Sally and me standing there.

"When I invited you guys to come I never thought in a million years that it was going to be the next day - and on Easter! Not only that, I initially did not recognize you yesterday. Then when I hopped back into the car, Pastor asked me if I knew who I was talking to for so long. Only after he told me did I realize why you looked so familiar."

Pastor Boone followed a few minutes later and had an equally shocked look on his face. Both reactions are priceless jewels in my heart to this day.

During the service, the youth choir had a special Easter number that they sang. I was pleasantly surprised to see that, during the number, they performed a beautiful choreographed dance built around sign language. I understood sign language from having to learn it in order to communicate with my niece, Monique, who was deaf. Her life was tragically cut short a few years before, when she was killed walking home from a night at the movie theater with her friends. The message they signed was beautiful. Instantly, my spirit was no longer troubled with Monique's death. Afterwards, I told Theresa that I was impressed with the youth choir's knowledge of sign language. Theresa shocked me when she said that they did not know sign language. How could this be? They signed several perfectly coherent sentences. Just as in the second chapter of the book of Acts, each person in his own tongue heard the apostles' messages, certainly the Holy Spirit could inspire an utterance in sign language, too. We both realized what had just happened, and the special Easter gift given to me suddenly all made sense.

Our friendship with the Boones and their entire congregation grew deep roots over the years with frequent visits to each others churches and other social events. One such event was their annual Brotherhood awards dinner. We had to miss several over the years because it coincided with my vacation, but there was one year where they had an unusual interest in my family's attendance. I gave it no second thought beyond the fact that it had been a little while since we had seen one another. Toward the end of the awards ceremony, Pastor Boone took the podium to announce the recipient of an extra special award. Pastor Boone began to spin a story that sounded far too familiar. I suddenly realized he was talking about me. Smiles broke out everywhere when the look on my face gave away my surprise. To be so loved by such a special congregation has empowered me like an eagle who is kept circling high, without effort, by the perpetual thermals.

There are very few awards adorning our home. My Brotherhood award is one of them because it reminds me of how rich I am for having the Covenant family as deeply loved friends. It sits between two other framed keepsakes, a photo of me and a friend with a former president, and my certificate of ordination from Grace Community Church in Massillon, Ohio, where another special friend is its founding pastor.

J. Michael Bragg

Dynamic and inexplicable things were happening in the mid-1990's not long after I responded to God's invitation to be part of something much larger than anything I had on my radar. Less than a year after enrolling in a distance seminary program through Southern Baptist Seminary in Nashville, I began receiving invitations to speak at area churches on Sunday morning, and at other faith-based functions during the week. If I had not recognized it as a door opened by God, I would have been puzzled by these invitations, since I never publicized any aspect of my academic pursuit. At one point, the invitations became so numerous, that I had to begin prioritizing them by time and distance with a focus on Sunday mornings.

One day, amidst the calls on my work voice mail, Pastor Michael Bragg from a church about an hour south of Cleveland called to extend an invitation to speak. After my breakfast break in between the morning and noon newscasts, I returned Pastor Bragg's call. When he answered my call, I had the immediate sense that I was speaking to someone I had known for a long time, yet it was the first time we had ever spoken to each other. I explained that I had to limit my speaking engagements for the time being to Sunday mornings in order to bring some stability to my schedule.

"Yes, that's exactly when we'd like for you to come," responded Pastor Bragg. Together, we looked over our desk planners and settled on a Sunday.

The drive down to Massillon from Geauga County included a stretch of road on which Sally and I had never traveled. Route 21 was surprisingly rural with rolling hills and occasional sprawling pastures. The scenery evoked silent worship, a perfect way to prepare to bring the message to a congregation that did not exist a handful of years before.

Pastor Mike met us at the door. It was the first time we had met face to face, but I would have recognized his smile anywhere since that very smile broke through with almost every word he had spoken on the phone. Before settling into his office, he showed us through the old church building they had purchased in 1990. He then started telling us about how, two years prior to that, God stirred his heart to head north to Ohio while he was the senior pastor of a church in North Carolina. It seemed like such an odd thing to do, but being obedient to this Divine stirring, he resigned his pastorate, packed their belongings and drove north without any idea of where specifically they were going. As they started running lean on the number of Ohio miles that they could go before driving into Lake Erie, they stopped in Massillon, just west of Canton. This is where God has led them to plant a new church from scratch. Amazingly, only two years later, they had a committed group of people who had formed a church so financially sound that they were able to purchase the old stone church.

We stepped into his office and I immediately felt at home as he asked about my faith journey. While I was happy to fill him in, I was more curious about why he would call me to share a message from the Ohio pulpit to which he was called. The answer should not have surprised me. He said that while he watched me deliver the forecast one day, his spirit was stirred to call me and invite me down to speak. As he spoke, I experienced the same ethereal awareness that I did while I was seated in Dick Lee's office at WCRF while speaking to Bob Devine. For only the second time in my life, I could see the unmistakable radiance of Christ beaming through the earthly servant that was drawn to move far away from home, to pastor a church that did not yet exist. There was an instant bond.

My journey has been filled to overflowing with family and friends that possess the kind of integrity that comes from a place outside themselves, but only twice up to this point has that manifestation been so compelling.

Pastor Mike quickly became one of several very important spiritual mentors to me during my second collegiate season, this time with a focus on Biblical studies. Even though he was a valued resource in that endeavor, more importantly, he became a close friend who joined the very small, exclusive core of men who came to know me as well as anyone could this side of eternity. One of our favorite lunch rendezvous is at a place called Macaroni's in Akron. Aside from the outstanding chicken cannelloni that we both ordered every time without ever looking at the menu, time seemed to move far too quickly as we talked like two old ladies rocking on the front porch for hours.

As I approached the last few classes in my seminary work, Pastor Mike asked me if I had considered being ordained. Even though I was only a few classes away from completing the program, I felt as if I were still ill-equipped for such a reverent event. It was my desire to cross the academic finish line first, but I tucked Pastor Mike's query into a corner of my heart like a seed that needed to be planted in order for germination to occur.

In the meantime, my brother Denié asked me if I would officiate at his wedding a few months away. I was honored, but had to find out what the Rhode Island state requirements were in order to have the authority to solemnize a wedding. After a few calls, I found out that the officiant had to either be an ordained minister or a church elder. I was still several years away from ordination and though I had served as an elder at a church just months before, my term concluded when we believed that we were being called to Fellowship Bible Church in Chagrin Falls. There was a third option. I could get special legislation passed in the state House of Representatives and Senate, then signed by the Rhode Island governor granting me the authority to perform a wedding ceremony. It was the only avenue available.

After several more calls, I finally spoke with the Rhode Island Senator who served Newport, where the wedding was scheduled. After hearing my story, Senator Cicilline agreed to try to find a co-sponsor for such a bill, but warned that trying to get the bill passed through the House in time would be difficult since they were on a two-week recess, not to mention getting the bill to the Governor's desk for a signature. Despite the odds, he seemed genuinely excited about trying to accomplish something much more fun compared to haggling budget numbers, or other routine legislative matters.

The ball was rolling, but I warned Denié that the chances of having all of the pieces come together were exceedingly small. Contacting a local justice of the peace, or another local pastor, should be arranged as a safety net.

The following week, Senator Cicilline introduced the bill with Senator Goodwin as the co-sponsor on March 30, 2000. It passed without effort. With the wedding now only twenty-eight days away, we had to wait another two weeks for the Rhode Island House to reconvene. Senator Cicilline gave me the web site address of the state House so I could keep an eye on their daily docket. He mentioned the bill to some of his friends serving as state legislators so that it would have a better chance of getting noticed. As the House convened two weeks before the wedding, I diligently checked their docket which was posted daily. Each day netted the same disappointing result. Two days before the wedding, the docket was full of bills scheduled to come to the floor, but once again the one bill I had hoped to see was absent. I called Denié and told him that the backup officiant would likely be performing their ceremony. At least we had had great fun trying to do what seemed like the impossible.

The next day, Denié called me in the afternoon. He was so excited that I could hardly understand him. The tale that he began to spin had me speechless. During his afternoon rounds as an ultrasound scanner at a Massachusetts hospital, he started casual conversation with one of the patients that he was scanning. It was unusual for him to share much about himself, but for whatever reason, Denié shared the story of his upcoming wedding, and how I was going to perform the ceremony, but could not because the special legislation needed never made it to the House floor.

The patient strained hard to get a look at his name tag. When he could not, the patient asked, "What is your name again?"

"Denié. Denié Bernier."

"You're the guy! You're the guy we've been talking about all day. I'm a state representative for the state of Rhode Island. One of the senators has been asking if his bill made it to the floor of the state house. Hold on."

While my brother was still scanning him, the legislator pulled out his cell phone and with urgency in his voice began firing off directives.

"Find the Cicilline bill. It has to be in that stack somewhere. Find it and get it to the floor of the House for a vote before the session wraps up. Hurry. We have less than an hour."

Denié had just witnessed Divine intervention. What was a Rhode Island legislator doing in a Massachusetts hospital? Out of all the ultrasound scanners available that day, how was it that the legislator walked into *his* office? Why did he open up and talk about his personal story to a perfect stranger, and tell him enough to trigger an important connection? It was all too surreal. The odds that every piece of that complex puzzle would come together in such a precise fashion had to be astronomical, beyond coincidence. The legislator released a firestorm of excitement through the state House as everyone was now scrambling to find the bill before that day's session was over. After his scan, he wished Denié well and disappeared into the crowded hospital hallway.

My goosebumps had goosebumps as I listened to how the story unfolded. Too much had been Divinely orchestrated to see it all fall apart at the very end. How it was going to get to the Governor's desk in time was still a mystery, but everything that happened that afternoon pointed to another miracle still waiting to unfold.

The next day, Sally and I were on a mid-afternoon flight to Providence. After landing, we wasted no time in picking up our rental car and starting the short drive to Newport where the wedding party was getting ready. Up to that point, there was no word whether or not the bill found its way to the House floor for a vote, let alone getting the Governor's signature.

Everyone was beginning to arrive. The justice of the peace was there waiting. After several failed attempts at calling Senator Cicilline, and with ten minutes left before the wedding was scheduled to begin, I tried calling the Senator one more time. This time, Senator Cicilline answered his phone.

"Hi Senator Cicilline. This is André Bernier. I'm in Newport and the wedding ceremony is scheduled to begin in ten minutes. Did the bill make it to the floor of the House?"

I waited what seemed like a small eternity for his response.

"André, the House staff searched high and low for my bill after getting a call from the legislator that your brother met. They finally found it. It was sitting at the bottom of a monster stack of things that needed to be considered. With minutes to spare, it was rushed to the floor for a vote and it was passed."

"What about the Governor's signature?" I asked.

"This is where it gets interesting. Somehow, the whole story of how the bill found its way to the floor reached the ears of the Governor. He was so moved by it, that he asked someone to bring it to his residence that evening so he could sign it into law. You're good to go, André. Congratulations. Have a wonderful evening, and a wonderful wedding for your brother."

"How can I ever thank you, Senator?" I asked.

"Believe me when I say that it truly was a pleasure to be a small part of such a series of miracles."

Except for my wife, my brother, and his wife-to-be, not a single invitee was aware of the possibility that I would preside over the wedding. The look on my family's face as I proceeded to the front and began the ceremony was truly priceless. Even better was the honor of joining my brother and his bride in Holy Matrimony, my first wedding as a minister. The carefully crafted inspirational message I intended to give during the ceremony went out the window, replaced by a completely ad lib story of the string of miracles that made this day possible. Denié and his bride, Stephanie, agreed that a story like this needed to be shared with everyone in attendance.

Several years later, my seminary work was complete. It was time. Pastor Mike asked me to send him a list of ordained ministers who were very familiar with my ministry work, so that he could assemble an ordination council. He also gave me the privilege of suggesting the individual who had, up to that point, mentored and influenced me the most, to be the council chairman. Without hesitation, senior pastor Jamie Rasmussen at our home church came to mind. Out of all the pastors with whom I have had the privilege of working over the last few decades, he was one of the few who immediately recognized my strengths and passions, and enthusiastically integrated them into his ministry blueprint for Fellowship.

Friday, May 21, 2004, was one day before my forty-fifth birthday. Six local pastors were scheduled to come together in Massillon at 6:00 P.M. for the ordination council. Earlier that morning, I had my hands full at the station tracking three intense clusters of severe weather. One of those clusters came through the night before, and another one came flying in during the morning rush hour. These were not run-of-the-mill thunderstorms. Each careened through with hurricane force winds and intense rain causing pockets of damage. At the end of my work day at noon, the sun was out and it looked like it was going to be a lovely day, but the third and most intense cluster was speeding toward Cleveland. The evening crew would have to deal with it. My mind was on being prepared for the council.

Since several of the pastors were from Fellowship, we arranged to meet so that we could car pool down to Massillon, about an hour and a half south. The air was hot and humid, and the sun was now veiled by a thick haze. Anyone could sense that the atmosphere was angry again as the clouds bubbled together and became dark. Pastor Jamie and Fellowship's founding pastor, Lud Golz and I piled into a car and began the drive south. While they began preparing me for the kinds of deep and introspective questions that I would be fielding, I couldn't help noticing that the next cluster of storms was making the sky turn black. My gaze was now fixed on what I believed was a wall cloud, the kind of cloud from which tornadoes form. Sensing my alarm, Pastor Lud asked if that looked menacing to me.

Still fixed on the sky, and with uneasiness in my voice, I piped up, "Oh, yes. In fact, I would be prepared to pull over quickly. There may be a tornado trying to form."

While a tornado did not form, we slowed down to a crawl on the highway as we hit a wall of water accompanied by wind that was so powerful it pushed Pastor Lud's car vigorously from side to side. Tree branches flew by like feathers in a breeze. Pieces of hail pinged on the roof and windshield. It was as if the agents of hell were doing everything possible to prevent us from getting to Massillon. Everyone in the car was quiet until the worst of the wind, rain and hail was over.

Some time later, we pulled into the church parking lot. Even though we were a few minutes late, no one else had yet arrived. That did not surprise any of us since we encountered gridlock at many intersections where traffic lights had lost power. We wondered if anyone else would show. Slowly, one by one, those invited to participate in the council arrived and soon there was a quorum.

When I initially considered enrolling in seminary, I had an uncommonly vivid dream in which, three times, I was reminded that ministry work was not a game. Three times I responded the same way.

"Yes, I know."

That came back to me as I engaged this council of pastors, many with whom I had served in ministry in various capacities. This was not a game. This was serious business. Many of the questions posed by my mentors were so deep and so probing, that it took every ounce of energy I had to answer them. In some cases, I had to dig for the answers from a deep part of the soul that an average person would hardly ever visit. I actually learned a great deal about myself that evening, and was truly grateful to have gone through something so intense. By the time I left the conference room so that they could enter into their deliberations, I was physically exhausted. It felt as if I had emptied my inner core out on the table, and the only thing that walked out of the conference room was a shell of a man running on fumes.

One of two pastors who were not there for the council arrived exceedingly late due to the snarled traffic everywhere. I told him that the council had just ended with the inquiry, and had just started deliberations. When he went inside, they warmly invited him to participate. The door closed once more, and it was dark and quiet. When it reopened, Pastor Jamie came out to offer his congratulations on the council's unanimous recommendation for ordination.

People began to arrive and assemble in the church's sanctuary for the anticipated ordination service. Even longtime friend and former co-worker, Mark Koontz, made special arrangements to finish his production work in Florida, so that he could board an early flight home to Ohio to be with me. There were two things that were indelibly impressed on my memory from the service itself. The first was being surrounded by the people I loved, my extended family and close friends, sharing a defining moment in my journey. The second happened when all of the pastors were called forward for the traditional, Biblical practice of the laying on of hands. Out of reverence, my eyes were closed, my head bowed, and my hands were out in front of me with my palms facing up. As each pastor offered a prayer of commissioning, I felt the hands of another gently pressing against mine as I heard the powerful words from one of my mentors. I wondered whose hands they were since the pastor speaking behind me and to my right could not have been the one whose hands I felt. I slowly opened my eyes. In amazement, I saw no other hands touching mine, even though I still felt something. Immediately after the prayer concluded, the hands touching mine slowly lifted.

The same thing happened only one other time in my life. Once again, it revolved around a time of group prayer. A group of twelve came together for the sole purpose of praying for an outreach event at Fellowship at which my wife, Sally, was the invited speaker the following week. During that prayer time, once again I felt hands press against my open palms. I recognized it as being the same gentle hands that pressed against mine during the ordination service years before. Again, I opened my eyes and saw nothing. This time, I smiled and realized that they were the hands of the One who invited me to a delightful detour in life's journey, with the promise that He would walk with me every step of the way until the day we see each other face to face.

Topic Of The Town

Our son, Noah, was three and a half years old when we packed our new Subaru Outback, and headed for the mountains of northern New England for a Christmas vacation. It was the year

2000, and it was the very first time that the three of us would spend Christmas away from our extended families.

We left before dawn on that Friday morning before Christmas, trying to outrun a snowy system that was due to add more snow to the already impressive snow pack there. Taking the back way into the White Mountains, we stopped in St. Johnsbury, Vermont, for fuel and snacks as night was falling. For a brief moment while waiting for the fuel dispenser to click, it felt as if I were a student returning to Lyndon State, which was only ten miles north. All it took was a glance at my wife and son in the car to remind me that twenty years had passed since then. Even so, it just seemed wrong not to drive by the campus, even though it was deserted for Christmas break. The snow suddenly became heavy and that was enough to convince me to forgo the academic detour.

Getting to Waterville Valley, New Hampshire, was no easy task. The seasonal shortcut road was closed due to deep, unplowed snow. The alternate route added an extra hour to our journey. By the time we reached our condo, we were all tired, cold and hungry. While Sally and I unpacked and started making dinner, our three-and-a-half year old son went on a mission. He searched every room and every closet until he found the item that had recently given him fascination, the vacuum cleaner. We plugged it in for him, and he quickly contributed by making certain the condo was clean. Every square inch of the carpet was done before dinner.

Over the next few days, our time introducing Noah to skiing met a serious challenge. The snow was not the issue. There was more than plenty. It was the brutally cold air. The strong winds added insult to injury by dishing out dangerously low wind-chill temperatures, along with the constant barrage of blowing snow. I thought for certain that Noah's first exposure to skiing would forever leave a bad taste in his mouth, and that skiing would never have any appeal. (I'm glad that I was wrong, but only after wisely waiting another five years to reintroduce it.)

On Christmas Eve the winds died down enough for us to plan on a Christmas Eve sleigh ride through the snowy woods. We prepared with untold layers from head to toe. By the time we walked out the door to walk to the town square, we looked like a family of life-sized marbles. When we arrived at the town square to await the arrival of the horse-drawn sleigh, we met up with a handful of other couples who would be joining us. They could have easily appeared on the cover of any fashion magazine. They were dressed in chic, colorful and form fitting apparel with very few layers. Those who wore hats did so for fashion, and not warmth.

Surely they had to have chuckled to themselves when they saw three life-sized marbles waiting for the sleigh with them. I looked over at the giant thermometer in the town square. It read ten degrees below zero. This was going to be an interesting ride.

The sleigh arrived with its driver and beautiful horses, adorned with the customary sleigh bells singing their rhythmic song with each step. Even though it was clear and starry, tiny ice crystals spontaneously sublimated in the air and, like snow, slowly settled to the ground. Sally and I had both seen this before in northern Vermont when temperatures fell well below zero, but it was the first time Noah had ever seen snow crystals falling from a totally clear sky. It was like Christmas Eve magic.

As the horses pulled us from the town square and deeper into the woods, the driver began to lead us into joyful choruses of "Winter Wonderland" and "Let It Snow." Parts of the path were beautifully decorated by small luminaries that served as a guide for the sleigh driver until we broke out into a wide farm field. Even though it was a moonless night, the brilliance of the stars and Milky Way actually provided enough light so that we could see its subtle features. It was more Christmas magic.

Sally, Noah and I were too occupied drinking in the glory of creation to notice that the once animated group with whom we were riding was getting very quiet. No longer were they excitedly moving about to look in every direction. Couples were now tightly huddled together trying to generate a little warmth. By the time the sleigh slid back into the woods, we started hearing teeth chattering, and soft murmuring about how cold it was getting.

Our driver asked if anyone wanted to sing another song, but the group did not respond. Sally, Noah and I were quite toasty, but we did not want to be the only ones singing. Our once exuberant and carefree sleighmates were now focused only on returning to the town square as quickly as possible, while the three life-sized marbles were hoping that time would stand still for just a few more moments. As beautiful as the stars looked, and as still as the air stood, it was difficult to imagine that another storm was looming.

After a wonderful night's sleep dreaming about our storybook Christmas Eve sleigh ride in the snowy woods, we awoke to an cacophony of strange sounds on Christmas morning. With eyes half open, we began to wander from our bedrooms to look out the living room window. We saw nothing but a wall of white, swirling past a window that was mostly obscured by pasted snow and ice. Several wind gusts made ear-piercing whistles that made us stand back, wondering if the window could take the powerful gusts. We were thankful that we had planned to stay in our cozy and warm cocoon for our Christmas breakfast.

By mid-morning, the sun broke out, but the wind insisted on whipping up frequent walls of blowing snow all the more. It was also clear that the sun would do little to coax thermometers out of below-zero territory. This was pure arctic air straight from the bowels of the north pole. We doubted that many people would try out their new Christmas skis.

Despite the inconceivable wind chill temperatures, we proceeded to get ready for a drive into the valley, hoping to find a Christmas Day church service to attend. The air was so cold that the heat coming from the vents of the car was tepid at best, but at least it prevented frost from forming on the inside of the windows.

By the time we drove around and located a few of the churches in the valley, many of the services were either well underway or already dismissed. At that point, we decided to do some exploring. Pointing the car back to the north, we headed for Franconia Notch and watched as the outdoor temperature indicator on the dashboard begin to go down into below-zero territory once more, as our elevation and the snow depth increased. Our destination was a little village called Bethlehem, so named because its name was selected on Christmas Day in 1799. We wanted to be able to tell family and friends that we had gone to Bethlehem for Christmas Day.

When we arrived, we were greeted by roads that were deep with a foot of new, unplowed snow, and several other feet of old snow on everything else. Our tire tracks were the only ones on any road we took. Bethlehem was eerily serene. If it were not for the smoke coming out of chimneys on the old, stately homes, we might have thought that we were the only ones alive for miles. We felt like we were experiencing the inside of a giant, isolated snow globe in an episode of the Twilight Zone.

Hunger pangs began to remind us that it was well past lunchtime. Since we were not exactly driving through a metropolis, heading to the biggest town would give us the best chance of finding a place of business that was open. Littleton was only five miles away, but because the road from Bethlehem to Littleton was largely unplowed, it felt more like twenty. Thankfully, we were driving our Subaru Outback. Just like in the hamlet of Bethlehem, most of the time our deeply-carved tire tracks were the only ones on the road.

Finally arriving in Littleton, we began looking for places of business that might be open. A McDonald's sign appeared in the distance. We drove toward the fast food restaurant, but I already knew from my six years of working there that McDonald's was typically closed on two days of the year - Thanksgiving Day and

Christmas Day. As I suspected, the parking lot was as empty as all of the roads.

I had one more idea. Surely there was a convenience store that would be open for a few more hours. We all looked for a 7-Eleven or a Cumberland Farms. Finally, the familiar Cumberland Farms logo was visible down Meadow Street. We could at least put something together that would tide us over, so that we could return to the ski area and make Christmas dinner. Our hearts dropped when we saw yet another empty parking lot and dark storefront. Even Cumberland Farms was closed for Christmas.

We were all becoming hungry and irritated. I suggested driving down Main Street at least once to see if there was any sign of activity anywhere before heading back to the condo, which was at least an hour away. As we drove through the mainly deserted downtown district, I immediately noticed a string of parked cars ahead that seemed to be concentrated in one area. We drove past once, and while looking left saw what appeared to be a diner that was open. A free-standing sandwich board indicated that it was a free Christmas dinner. I turned around and looked for a parking spot. Sally was skeptical, thinking that the dinner was either a private affair, or for those considered homeless. I wasn't convinced of either conjecture. It was time for a reconnaissance mission.

With the car still running so that Sally and Noah would not get cold, I ran several business doors down Main Street and walked into Topic Of The Town restaurant. Immediately greeted by a delightful hostess, I simply asked if they were open for lunch, to which she replied, "Oh absolutely. Come on in, find a spot to sit down and help yourself to our Christmas buffet."

"Well, my wife and son are waiting in the car."

"By heavens, go and bring them in too!"

Running back to the car was more painful since I was now running into the icy wind. As I approached the car, and as tears were streaming from my eyes from the extreme cold, I motioned for Sally and Noah to come.

Sally opened the car door, "So what's the deal?"

"I don't know. All I know is that they are open and there is food."

All three of us made a mad dash for the diner. The hostess was there waiting for us, and made us feel as if we were family. She offered to take our coats, but we were all still so cold that we wore them to the roomy table to which she brought us. She pointed to the buffet and told us to grab a plate and to enjoy whatever we wanted with their compliments. A lovely waitress came by and asked us what we wanted to drink, and brought the drinks to the table. We walked toward a man with a tall chef's hat sharpening his knife behind one of the biggest steaming turkeys we had ever seen.

This was no ordinary buffet. It was a feast the likes of which we had trouble comprehending. As the chef sliced the turkey for our plates, he told us that it was only one of many turkeys that had already been carved and served in the last few hours. Mashed potatoes, marshmallow sweet potatoes, homemade stuffing and gravy, corn on the cob, green beans and fluffy dinner rolls were also waiting to find a home on our plates.

"Save room for dessert," he proclaimed with a smile, while he pointed to yet another table with various pies, cakes and other sweet Christmas treats.

The meal was outstanding. Better still was that we knew that we were welcomed guests, even though we were complete strangers who had never stepped into the Topic Of The Town restaurant until that day.

As Sally and Noah scanned the dessert table for a Christmas treat, I spotted the chef who had served us our turkey in the middle of the restaurant with his hands on his hips. His stately body language had presence, and confirmed to me that this was the owner of the restaurant. I approached him to introduce myself, and to tell him our story. Finding Topic Of The Town was nothing short of God's answer to our predicament.

The owner, Dennis Fekay, told me that it all started sixteen Christmases before, when his daughter came home from school asking if they could hold a free community Christmas dinner as a part of a school project. The family rallied around the idea. By Christmas Day, 1985, the word was out. Any person who did not want to eat Christmas dinner alone was encouraged to come to the restaurant, and enjoy Topic Of The Town's free community Christmas dinner. About thirty people showed up to that first dinner. At the end of the day, the Fekay family realized that it was a wonderful way to express their thanks to a community that supported their business throughout the year.

I asked, "Dennis, is there any way that I can pay for our meal today?"

"What part of 'free' don't you understand? It's our way of saying 'thank you' to everyone."

"But we're not a part of your community."

"You are now."

While there was never any charge for anyone who came through their restaurant doors on Christmas Day, anyone who insisted on reciprocating in a monetary fashion could place their money in a basket, and that would then be donated to a local charity. They never took a penny.

Even though we lived in Cleveland, Ohio, the Fekay family kept in contact with us, especially at Christmas time. It has always been our custom to send a donation to their Christmas Day kitty that they send to a charity.

The Topic Of The Town's annual Christmas dinner, born in a young girl's heart, has now grown into a well-attended and greatly-loved event in Littleton. In a hand-written letter that Dot mailed to us last Christmas, she wrote:

"Dear André and family,

"It means so much to us to hear from you. We look forward to this every year.

"We are so busy with the restaurant, and catering Christmas parties, and now getting ready for the annual Christmas dinner. We haven't had the chance to go through the package you sent. We will after Christmas. You are just awesome folks. Merry Christmas.

"Bless you, Denny and Dot."

Rarely have I experienced such extravagant generosity, which was a real answer to our desperate prayer. I'm convinced that the events of our day were Divinely directed, so that we could not only enjoy their special gift to us, but to witness the way this restaurant family loves the people that God places in their path. That day gave us some new "forever friends." It also gave me a life lesson that continues to minister to me today.

Epilogue

In many ways, it seems rather odd to end here. Every time that I wrapped up painting a story with words, I would think of another, and another. Finding a logical place to retire the paintbrush was difficult. My longtime friend, Hollywood director Jason Tomaric, told me that knowing when to put the paintbrush down in a creative work was just as important as the content of the work itself. As a writer, filmmaker, and even television meteorologist, Jason taught me an important principle that will prevent me from messing up a good thing. This is where I am putting my paintbrush down.

Assuming I live to the ripe old age of one hundred, I still have roughly half of life's journey ahead. Even if I have overestimated my earthly timeline, I am looking forward to many more delightful encounters with the people I know and love, and those I have yet to meet. I'm certain I will glean something from each one.

Whether your name has been mentioned in this book or not, trust me, if our paths have crossed, even for a moment, you have enriched my journey like a field of wildflowers that border life's footpath.

Time has been a wonderful teacher as well. Living out stories in the undercurrent of time has led me to an important revelation: The people with whom I have had the pleasure of "doing life" are my most treasured possessions. Do not misunderstand me. People are not possessions like a car or a plane. The possessions of which I speak are these unique friendships whose worth is incalculable. I am truly rich beyond rich because of each person with whom I have shared even the smallest portion of the footpath.

My friend Jon Loufman, a talented Cleveland meteorologist, has a wonderful perspective on our earthly journey. He said that, in the grand scheme of things, it is like going through the thinnest sheet of paper you could imagine. Once life reaches its inevitable conclusion, you break through that very thin sheet. Now you have the vastness of the remainder of the universe ahead, which is only the beginning of eternity. It will truly take all of eternity for me to express my gratitude to God for using so many people to teach me His ways.

May you too see every person as a treasured gift...

...especially those who have gone the extra mile.